Second Chance

Second Chance

The heartwarming true story of a neglected horse who became a Mounted Police hero

DIANA THURGOOD

ALLEN&UNWIN
SYDNEY • MELBOURNE • AUCKLAND • LONDON

First published in 2024

Allen & Unwin
Cammeraygal Country
83 Alexander Street
Crows Nest NSW 2065
Australia
Phone: (61 2) 8425 0100
Email: info@allenandunwin.com
Web: www.allenandunwin.com

Allen & Unwin acknowledges the Traditional Owners of the Country on which we live and work. We pay our respects to all Aboriginal and Torres Strait Islander Elders, past and present.

A catalogue record for this book is available from the National Library of Australia

ISBN 978 1 76106 888 1

Set in 12.65/19.75 pt Bembo Std by Midland Typesetters, Australia
Printed and bound in Australia by the Opus Group

10 9 8 7 6 5 4

The paper in this book is FSC® certified. FSC® promotes environmentally responsible, socially beneficial and economically viable management of the world's forests.

They say that 'beauty is in the eye of the beholder'. That 'it's what's on the inside that counts'. They also say that 'beauty is only skin deep'. In fact, there are a whole range of platitudes that are meant to make those born less than perfect feel better about themselves. But it is not that easy when society constantly makes judgements about value based only on attractiveness.

This is a true story of one woman's kindness, one horse's courage and their ultimate triumph against all odds.

Contents

Part 2: Saving Tiff

Note on horse terminology

Sexes

A stallion is an adult male and a mare is an adult female; horses are considered adult at three years of age. Colt and filly are the respective terms for young horses. A gelding is a neutered male.

Measurements

Horses are measured to their wither (the bump, just in front of where a saddle is placed, where their neck joins their back) in hands. One hand is 4 inches (about 10 centimetres). A horse is taller than 14.2 hands (147 centimetres); shorter horses are called ponies.

Colour and body

A bay horse has a brown coat, with a black mane, tail and legs. The leg markings may be very short, barely reaching above the hoof, or they can extend to the top of the leg.

A horse's conformation refers to its physical shape, and how well that conforms to an ideal type.

'Feathers' are the extra-long hairs that grow around the back part of the lower legs of heavy horse breeds, such as Clydesdales.

A coronet band is the area between the hair on the horse's lower leg and start of the hoof wall.

A fetlock is the horse equivalent of a human ankle.

Training

Starting and breaking are interchangeable terms used to describe the process of training a horse to be ridden.

A green-broken horse is one that has been started or broken to saddle and bridle but has not been ridden much.

Collection describes when a horse shifts its centre of gravity backwards so that it bears more of its own weight and that of its rider in its hindquarters rather than its shoulders. A collected horse elevates its head and neck, thereby giving its front legs and shoulders more freedom to move. Collection not only allows the horse to move more easily and athletically, but also helps prevent wear and tear on the front legs. Teaching a horse to collect itself is part of training.

Miscellaneous

Agistment is a paddock or stable where a horse is kept for a fee.

Floating boots are a set of four protective coverings that are placed around the horse's legs to protect them when floating/transporting.

A headstall, also called a halter or head collar, is the part of a bridle that encircles the horse's head.

Knackery and doggers are both terms used to describe a slaughterhouse or a place where old, infirm and unwanted horses are killed for dogfood. The term dogger is also used to describe a buyer of these horses.

Tack is a general term used to describe the equipment or accessories used for riding or general management of horses and includes saddles, bridles, stirrups, headstalls.

PART 1
Saving Toby

'The idea that some lives matter less is the root of all that is wrong with the world'

Paul Farmer

CHAPTER 1

The horse in the dusty paddock

January 2001

Someone must have opened the gates of hell. A blast of torturous heat blew across the yard and suffocating red dust rose up and filled his lungs. A swarm of flies lingered around his eyes, the inflammation causing tears that leaked down his cheeks in a dark river. He cowered under a sickly tree, the only shade in this baking prison, thinking of nightfall and waiting for the relief it would bring. A few thistles were growing in the paddock, but they offered no nourishment, and his water trough was slimy and tepid. Once a day, a biscuit of rough, burry hay was thrown into his paddock and although it hurt his mouth, he ate it hungrily. His coat was parched and dirty, his hooves were cracked and long but probably the most haunting thing about him was his eyes. At first glance, they looked empty and lifeless, yet if you looked closer, you could see the disappointment and despair as well as resignation and defeat.

He looked old, a broken-down old nag who'd seen better days. But he was young—barely eighteen months old and this was the only life he knew.

On the other side of the fence, another horse thrived, his muscles and veins bursting with vitality. His every move was poised, and he displayed an arrogance that is typical of the very young. His coat was satin, glistening with a slight film of sweat, and his muscles rippled as he moved.

He was not hungry, he had plenty to eat and a shed for shelter. His water trough was clear and refilled daily. He had no reason to doubt that any of these essentials would be provided and with this faith came the luxury of play. He cantered effortlessly around the paddock. He was stunning. A gorgeous specimen of a horse with excellent conformation and a beautiful head.

The attractiveness of a horse's head is a matter of personal choice but generally a horse, especially a show horse, should have one that is in proportion to its body. It should not be coarse but by the same token, it should not be weak. Arab and part-bred Arabs have a slightly dished or concave face while draft horses typically have a roman nose. This is where the face is convex—sloping gently outwards from the forehead and then tapering back in towards the nose. While a roman nose is acceptable in heavy workhorses, it is usually not desirable in other breeds, although some people are not bothered by it at all.

The horse in the dusty paddock was a well-bred horse. He stood an impressive 15.2 hands and was the result of a cross between a Clydesdale stallion and a Stockhorse mare. He was a rich bay in colour, had a calm, dependable nature, and displayed great intelligence. He did, however, have a roman nose.

The horse on the other side of the fence was also well bred. In fact, the two horses were half-brothers. This horse stood an impressive 16 hands and was jet black in colour. He too displayed great intelligence but did not have a roman nose.

This one cosmetic detail was the sole reason why the two horses experienced such startlingly different circumstances. One would be pampered, trained, and sold as a competition horse, while the other was destined for the knackery.

It was the year 2001 and the New South Wales country-side was in the grip of a horrific drought. Crops were failing and feed prices were exorbitant. Farmers were selling their stock and leaving the family farm forever. Sometimes the sale price of the animal did not even cover the cost of transport, so animals were shot where they stood, weakly, in the paddock. Even hobby farmers with secondary incomes could not afford to buy feed and were abandoning their farms in droves. It was not a time of sentimentality; it was a time of hard, cold, economic facts. Animals, even those who had once been treasured companions, were seen as liabilities to be off-loaded.

Gary, the owner of both horses, was faced with the same dilemma and, unable to feed even a single large horse, had decided to sell both. The good-looking one might bring a decent price from someone wanting to buy a dressage horse. The ugly one was simply not worth the risk. He would take longer to sell and may not sell at all. So, Gary put all his time, energy and resources into the good-looking horse.

It was not a difficult decision to make. He had no attachment to either horse, they were simply commodities to be bought and sold. One had the potential to create a return on his investment, the other did not.

People keep animals for all sorts of reasons: for work, prestige, profit and some simply because they love them. To these people the idea that you could lavish attention on one animal, yet neglect another's basic needs seems incomprehensible. They are connected to animals on an emotional level and are repulsed by any form of cruelty, neglect or mistreatment. In fact, some animal lovers are so highly tuned to animals that they can actually 'feel' their suffering and anguish.

Sadly, the chances of the neglected horse meeting such a person were remote. The property was isolated, and he was hidden out the back, away from view. So, he continued to live his wretched existence, day in and day out, slowly deteriorating and losing interest in everything around him. Luckily, he had no idea of what awaited him—a trip to the saleyards and then a sudden, bloody and violent end.

Meanwhile, the good-looking horse thrived. He received balanced meals and was wormed and groomed. Each day he was lunged on a long lead and learnt new commands. He enjoyed these sessions as he grew easily bored in the paddock and needed to work off his excess energy. By the end of each lesson, he was looking forward to some feed and a rest. His owner was experienced with horses and this combined with the young horse's intelligence meant he learnt quickly and easily. He did not care about the future; he was happy with the present. Either way, he was destined for great things.

But things do not always turn out as we expect. Sometimes a chance meeting or seemingly random incident can completely change a person's (or animal's) destiny. Unbeknown to the two horses, an event was about to occur that would change both their lives forever.

CHAPTER 2

A face only a
mother could love

Nambucca Heads was only three hours drive from the two
horses, but it may as well have been a world away. Green
rolling hills and subtropical forests gently merging with
golden beaches and crystal clear, blue water and a soothing
sea breeze made the nights brisk and comfortable.

Tiffany was holidaying at Jinki, her mother's farm on
the New South Wales north coast. An Indigenous name for
place of good spirits, Jinki radiated peace. Bathed in early
morning sunlight, the farmhouse was cosy and comforting.
It wasn't old but it was well lived in.

Tiff and her husband Col had driven up from Sydney one
week earlier to visit her mother Ann and enjoy some well-
earned rest and recreation. The sultry days were beginning

to take their toll on her motivation and stamina so she rose early, eager to go for a ride before the heat drained all her energy. She then planned to spend the afternoon lazing on the wisteria-laced veranda, thinking about her next great adventure. Her life was crazy and intense . . . just how she liked it. She just needed a little down time to process the massive changes that were about to take place in the next few months. If she could mentally prepare for them, then she knew she'd be just fine.

Tiff played absentmindedly with her long, thick, dark brown plait as she sat eating breakfast. Her hairstyle was unchanged since childhood. She liked her hair long and a plait kept it manageable. A few people had remarked that her hair reminded them of her horses' flowing manes and that maybe she subconsciously began to resemble the animals she admired so much. She found the idea amusing but didn't read too much into it. She didn't have time for hairstyles, make-up or clothes. There were way too many other important things to worry about.

Tiff picked up the local paper and turned a few pages, more out of habit than interest. There was the usual stuff: the local MP opening an art exhibition, the Surf Life Saving Club's annual fundraising dinner, the district sports results and the classifieds.

Tiff was the sort of person who found it impossible to drive past a garage sale or auction and the newspaper's classifieds were no exception. She was a self-confessed bargain hunter and found great joy in sharing her purchasing triumphs with anyone who would listen.

While the classifieds usually attracted her interest, on this morning something was different. As she scanned the columns, she felt like she was looking for 'something'. That there was something she needed to find. After a few moments, such a sense of urgency had consumed her that she didn't even notice her coffee had gone cold. She sat there sipping the tepid brew, eyes keenly focused, looking. Finally, amongst the farm machinery and fencing supplies, she found it.

A horse for sale.

Tiff was confused. She didn't need another horse; she already had two of her own. Maybe there was something else she was meant to find. She tried to move on, but her eye kept returning to the small classified ad.

Tiff's interest in horses was not just confined to riding or even competing. She had just been accepted into the New South Wales Mounted Police, so horses were a huge part of her life. Over the years she had bought and sold and trained many horses. She enjoyed it. She found horses uncomplicated, unlike most people. It was incredibly rewarding to take an unruly, unloved horse and help it reach its true potential then rehome it to a place where it was both wanted and cherished.

But all of that was in the past. Tiff knew the demands of her new role would seriously limit the time she had for her own horses, let alone taking on and training others. She put the paper down and poured another coffee, then returned to her seat. The new cup too went cold as she sat there lost in thought. Why the hell was she considering this horse? Sure, it was a good deal. An unbroken, black, Clydesdale-cross gelding, eighteen months old, for six hundred dollars. Even with the current drought, it was a good price and Clydie-crosses were her favourites.

Tiff reasoned that maybe in a year or so, things might have settled down. She would leave him to mature anyway. Then if at that point she still didn't have time for him, one of her friends would take him on and train him. Tiff and Col had their horse float with them as they had brought their two horses Ben and Samson, so she abandoned her plans for the rest of the day and decided that the gelding might be worth a look.

Col entered the kitchen and glanced at her. She had gone silent and looked distracted.

'Anything up?' he asked.

Tiff looked back at him and answered, 'You're not going to believe this.'

She picked up the phone and punched in the number. After only a few rings a man answered. Tiff explained that she was calling about the horse and he gave her some basic information.

'He'd make an excellent eventing horse, love. I could see that the moment I looked at him. So much presence and brave too. Never been sick in his life, great feet, good doer. You won't be disappointed, darlin'.'

The prattle sounded well rehearsed and a little too good to be true. Tiff also didn't like being called 'love' and 'darling' by someone she'd never met and it did little to build her confidence in the whole venture. Even as they hooked up the horse float, she wondered what on earth she was doing. It was one thing to be spontaneous and act on a whim. It was quite another to waste a tank of fuel and a whole day driving in the stinking heat.

But within an hour she and Col had set off, watching as the green pastures gave way to barren fields, and as their surroundings turned from paradise to hell.

The kilometres ticked over. The dust seeped in through the air vents and the sun beat through the windscreen unrelentingly. The road deteriorated the further they went along until Tiff felt it couldn't get any worse. Occasionally she would see a farmhouse and start to feel a sense of relief that maybe their nightmare journey was over, but it was never the right place, and they would drive on . . .

Tiff had a picture in her mind of the picturesque farm that they were heading to and the bright-eyed youngster who would meet them at the fence. But as they finally pulled in at the gate of the address she had been given, her hopes plummeted.

The place was a dump. There was litter everywhere. The old shed was filled to the brim with rubbish that cascaded out through the open doors. There were carcasses of old cars in various stages of disrepair and mangled sheets of iron stacked haphazardly in piles around the perimeter. The fences looked as though they were held together with baler twine. There was no lawn or shrubs and only a few trees to speak of. The paint was peeling off the house in ribbons and many of the windows were boarded up. Those with the glass still intact were dressed in faded floral bed sheets that flapped in the hot, dry wind. This was definitely not a good place to buy an animal and Tiffany cursed herself for her stupidity. She didn't even dare look over at Col.

Then she saw him. He walked out of the small, rusty corrugated iron shed and trotted over to the fence. The horse's owner arrived at exactly the same time, introducing himself simply as 'Gary'.

He was a short man with dark hair and cold, hard eyes. Tiff wasn't sure if it was the dust or that he normally wore a sour expression on his face but the deep crease lines on his brow seemed to indicate the latter. He was thin and wiry, possibly an ex-jockey, and was dressed in shorts, a singlet and a pair of non-matching thongs. He wore a trucker's cap and a cigarette dangled from his lips.

'Ah, I see you've met Bundy—I told you he was a beauty. I had big plans for this horse but the drought put that to shit.

Put a lot of things to shit really. And then me missus left me. Worthless piece of shit she was anyway. Better off without her, that's what everyone says. So I'm selling up and I've got a job in the mines. I bet she'll be begging me to take her back when she finds out how much money I'm making.'

Tiff stood open-mouthed. The onslaught of information and the attitude was just too much to bear. She wished he would leave them alone or at least shut up so that she could collect her thoughts but he continued on and on, about everything and nothing. Two minutes ago she was ready to get back in the car and drive home. Now she was torn. He really was a beautiful horse with so much potential but what an awful place, and God knows how he'd been treated. She decided to give him the benefit of the doubt, so she wrestled open the gate and walked into the paddock.

Bundy didn't flinch as she put her hand on his neck; in fact, he seemed quite relaxed. He turned to face her with a curious look and waited expectantly. She ran her hands over his back and down his legs while he stood quietly. She picked up each of his feet then checked between his legs, but as she did, he recoiled in fear.

Gary spoke up immediately. 'I only had him gelded yesterday, so there's another bonus.'

When Bundy had calmed down, Tiff opened his mouth and checked his teeth, which were fine; she decided his age was pretty spot-on. Things were definitely looking up. He was a good-looking young horse, in good condition with a nice nature. Tiff asked Gary for a lead and signalled to Col to take the rope. He set off with Bundy jogging along effortlessly behind him. When the pace quickened, Bundy broadened his step, showing no sign of weakness or lameness. They completed a circle in each direction then returned to the gate.

Gary, delighted at the outcome, jabbed Tiff excitedly in the arm. 'Marvellous isn't he, love? I told you he was a winner.' He then called out to Col: 'So are you going to break him in for the wifey?'

Col watched Tiff's face contort and choked back a laugh. 'Nah mate, she's the horse person. She's actually a Mountie,' he added proudly. Technically Tiff wasn't yet, but she had been accepted and was due to start with them in a month so that was good enough for Col.

A schoolboy smirk spread across Gary's face and he replied sleazily, 'I don't want to know about your sex life.'

'A mounted policewoman,' Col responded coolly.

'I thought they'd be men,' Gary replied, his eyes narrowing, obviously confused by the revelation.

'Actually, 75 per cent are women,' Tiff added.

Not knowing what to say, Gary said nothing but his contempt for the whole idea was palpable. When he regained his composure, he nudged Tiff again and added, 'There's a lot of people interested in him, so you're really getting a bargain here, darlin'.'

Tiff found it annoying that he already assumed she would buy the horse, even though in all likelihood she probably would. While there were plenty of outwardly irritating things about this man, Tiff also had a feeling that he wasn't as caring or jovial as he made out. She had always been very intuitive about people's natures and could usually tell when someone was false or fake. Gary's manner set off multiple alarm bells for her. The incessant chatter, the nervous laughter, his habit of constantly bringing every conversation back to himself . . . And now he was trying to rush her into a sale. Tiff was determined not to give in too easily and wanted to make him sweat a bit longer, so she asked to use the toilet. She noticed he stiffened momentarily, frowned, and then mumbled something about it being round the back of the house, the last door on the right.

She rounded the corner of the building and spotted the toilet door. A large, cross-breed dog sprawled lazily across the entrance and lifted its head as she approached, then laid it back down again, too hot to bother with her. The toilet was grimy and smelly but she realised that after three hours she really did need to go, so she went in and held her breath. There was a washbasin but the tap didn't work, so she went in search of a hose.

As she scanned the back of the property, she noticed another horse standing under a scrubby tree, his head almost touching the ground. His rib cage and hips protruded, and his gut was swollen and distended. She walked up to him and was almost upon him before he noticed her. He lifted his weary head and looked in her direction then slowly returned to his oblivion. There was no mistaking it: he too was a Clydesdale-cross but, unlike Bundy, definitely no beauty. Even apart from his emaciated condition, he was weirdly out of proportion. His head was large and ungainly, and he had a prominent roman nose.

Tiff looked at him with immense pity and reached out to steady herself after a wave of nausea washed over her. She had seen many things over the past three years in the Police Force: car accidents, domestic violence incidents, assaults. She had even found people who had been dead for several days. She had learned for her own sanity to partially switch off, to detach and to stay focused on her role: providing comfort and keeping people safe. But it was so hard when confronted with violence or neglect to children and animals. Their helplessness was harrowing. Their vulnerability cut to her core.

How could anyone let a horse get in this condition? The poor old thing should have been euthanised a long time ago.

Tiff stood there for a while trying to comprehend how two such vastly different horses could be on the same property, in such proximity. She also came to the sickening conclusion that she had been right about Gary. There was definitely another side to this man, possibly even darker than she had imagined.

As she stood there, burning with rage, Gary rounded the corner and approached. He looked annoyed when he saw Tiff in the horse's paddock but somehow managed to keep his temper in check.

'Ah, I see you've met Toby, a face only a mother could love. But then of course I'm not his mother,' he laughed.

Tiff tried to keep her voice flat and unemotional but it wavered, betraying her true intent. 'How old is he?' she asked.

Gary, too ignorant to notice the change in her demeanour, continued on answering light-heartedly, 'The same age as Bundy—actually they're half-brothers. I bought them both together but got duped with him, the bastard. Ugly son of a bitch.'

'So, you've decided to make him pay?' Tiff observed.

'Yeah, something like that,' Gary laughed.

Tiff looked at Toby. The name suited him. She could feel his sweetness. Somewhere hidden inside that hollow husk of a horse was a beautiful heart.

She couldn't stand the thought of this man getting away with animal abuse but with so many starving animals around, the chance of a conviction was negligible. Plus she didn't have a camera on her.

But she knew this was not simply a case of drought-affected starvation. Gary had consciously chosen to feed one horse but not the other. He obviously had the resources but had callously disregarded Toby's welfare based solely on his looks. It was sick and it was spiteful.

Standing there in silence, it finally began to dawn on Gary that perhaps Tiff didn't share his perspective or sense of humour and he started to get defensive. 'Well look at him—who would want that? It's a waste of money feeding him,' he spat out maliciously. 'Anyway, a truck's coming in the morning to take him to the knackers. So do you want this other horse or not?'

Tiff reluctantly left Toby and followed Gary back to Bundy. She reasoned that Toby would be long gone before the RSPCA would save him, if they could at all. She decided that she wanted to get as far away from this man and this place as possible, so she agreed to the $600 sale price and handed over the money. Gary's manner immediately improved, and he became jovial and light-hearted once again.

'That's wonderful, I'm sure you'll be very happy with him, love. You'll have to let me know how he goes. I'd be really interested to follow his progress.'

Tiff nodded although she had no intention of ever speaking to this man again. Why would she? He didn't care, and probably would never care, about his animals. She ignored Gary and instructed Col to back the float up.

Col and Tiff opened the back gate, and she took out a headstall and lead rope. She slipped it onto Bundy's head and walked him in a circle before approaching the ramp.

Bundy obediently put two feet up, then changed his mind, throwing up his head and pulling backwards.

No doubt the float looked strange and unfamiliar. It was no surprise that he would be reluctant, as it smelt of other horses. Col and Tiff persisted patiently. Losing their temper would just make things worse but they soon realised there was no way they were getting him on the float. A couple of times they got him halfway up the ramp but he always shot off sideways. Things were not looking good. They had been at it for over half an hour, and the heat and flies were taking their toll. Finally, Tiff asked for a bucket of feed to help entice him onto the float, but Gary replied that there was none.

'Ran out this morning. He was going to be sold, and the other thing's off to the knackery.'

Tiff stared at him uncomprehendingly. She couldn't believe she was buying a horse from someone like this. She couldn't even believe that she was here talking to him. In desperation, she unhooked the float, jumped in the car, and headed off to a town to buy a few bags of carrots and loaves of bread.

When Tiff returned, she was too angry, not with Bundy but with the whole sordid situation, to talk. She hooked up the float and gave Bundy a few carrots to win his interest, then resumed the task of getting him on the float. On the third attempt, they were successful. Col quickly put the bar behind his rump and fumbled with the bolt, managing to get it into place. Then they hoisted the back ramp. Bundy sensed he was trapped and started pulling backwards, pushing with all his might against the bar but it was too late. The ramp was almost in place and with some pushing and shoving it was finally shut and bolted and they both sighed in relief.

Finally, they could be on their way. Tiff picked up what was left of the carrots and loaves of bread and then remembered Toby. If Gary was telling the truth and there was no feed in the shed, then this poor, wretched animal would not have another meal for the rest of his miserable life. Tiff and Col walked towards the back paddock and opened the gate, despite Gary's protests.

'You should get going. It's getting late. What are you doing? That thing doesn't need any food. He's a brute, worst-tempered thing I've ever met . . . and ugly.'

Col and Tiff ignored him and walked to Toby, offering their gift. It was not much of a feed but more a symbolic gesture, that he may know some small act of kindness before he met his end. He took the food with the utmost grace and for a moment his eyes sparked with a hint of life. When the food was all gone, Toby nosed them gently and then, with the last of his energy, followed them unsteadily back to the gate, hoping for more. They walked away and never looked back. It was too painful.

Col and Tiff climbed into the car, started the engine, wound up the windows, and turned on the air conditioner. They drove out the gate watching Gary who stood there cheerfully waving them goodbye, like an old friend.

They drove in silence for a long time, listening to the banging in the horse float behind them. Neither of them knew what to say. They were both dumbfounded by what they had just experienced.

Finally, Col spoke up. 'We couldn't have got them both in the float anyway, we only just got Bundy in.'

Tiff agreed but it did little to lift her spirits and she couldn't get Toby out of her mind. 'How could someone do that?' she asked.

'You know as well as I do the sort of people there are in this world,' Col replied. She murmured in agreement.

Being a police officer, Tiff was privy to the best and worst society had to offer, but it still amazed her. She consoled herself with the fact that by the following day, Toby would at least be out of his misery. She hoped it would be a quick end and that he wouldn't suffer too much.

They started talking about other things in an attempt to forget him, but it was a half-hearted conversation and they eventually fell silent again. The trip home was slightly longer but it was late afternoon and at least they were not driving into the sun. They stopped to get some fuel and bought a few things to munch on, as neither of them had

had any lunch. Tiff eventually dozed off and only awoke as they were pulling into the driveway of Jinki.

They backed the float into the paddock and shut the gate. Bundy stamped noisily in protest. As expected, the moment the ramp was lowered and he was released, he shot out backwards, dragging Tiff a few metres before she managed to quieten him. She led him over to the water trough but he wasn't interested. There was too much newness around him and he was transfixed by the green grass beneath his feet. She unbuckled his headstall and for a moment he stood there, unsure of what to do. Suddenly he bolted, kicking and bucking across the paddock. He did a few circuits then pulled up heaving. Tiff called out to him and he set off again. When he eventually slowed down, he trotted over to them, stopping a short distance away. He dropped to his knees and rolled in the cool, green grass, rubbing his neck, head and back in sheer delight. He stood up and shook himself then was overtaken by another explosion of energy and galloped around before finally calming down and coming over for a pat.

Tiffany stood there looking at this beautiful horse, but suddenly the green paddock turned a blood red, and he morphed into Toby with his sunken eyes and swollen gut. She blinked and returned to the present but her mood had plummeted. The horses needed to be fed, the float had to be cleaned out and she longed for a shower. Surely, now she was home, she could forget about that other horse.

It wasn't to be. They had dinner, watched some television, and fell into bed exhausted but sleep didn't come easily. Tiff tossed and turned. Even though she had no accountability for Toby she still felt guilty. She suspected that no other person knew of his existence and hence no one else could save him. She was his only hope and it played with her heart and her head. Unwanted horses die every day, and you can't save them all. Even still, she had nightmares about him then, early in the morning, had a strange dream in which he was a magnificent horse, being admired and patted by hordes of strangers.

Tiff woke with an uneasy feeling. The dream was incredibly intense, albeit totally ridiculous, and she wasn't sure what it meant, if it meant anything at all. She looked over at Col and saw that he too had not slept well. Later that morning she realised she actually felt worse than she had the day before. Not so much physically, although she was still very tired, but mentally and emotionally drained. Worst of all she felt a deep sadness engulfing her. The type of sadness that turns your world grey and there is nothing you can do.

Well, there was one thing she could do . . .

CHAPTER 3

Toby

Go back and get him.

The thought played over and over in her mind.

Tiff couldn't believe she was considering it but the more she thought about it, the more sense it made. Sure, he would never be a show horse but he might make someone a nice, reliable trail horse. It actually didn't matter to her if she lost money on him; she just felt he deserved a chance. She figured if she left him here at Jinki for a year or two, then started him and did some basic education, she could easily sell him. Someone who wanted a quiet, sensible horse would quickly snap him up. She was planning on leaving Bundy here for a while anyway, so at least they'd be company for each other.

25

Col saw her approaching with a determined look on her face and knew exactly what she was going to say. 'Let me guess, you want to go back and get him. I was thinking the same thing.'

Tiff smiled in relief. 'And this is why I love you,' she said.

Col didn't want gratitude; he had been battling the same demons. He just wanted to be rid of the guilt so he said, 'Go and ring him, and I'll hook up the float.'

Tiff punched in the number. It rang and rang and just as she was about to hang up, Gary answered. He sounded surprised to hear from Tiff and spoke cautiously. 'Hi, how's he settled in?'

Tiff wasn't up for a chat, so she cut to the chase and explained that they had decided to come back today to buy Toby. They were prepared to pay saleyard or 'doggers' rate for him and she went on to say that he was only a young horse, in extremely poor condition and it was unlikely he would fetch any more than a hundred and fifty dollars.

Gary was surprised but agreed. 'Yes, I can see why you'd want him. He's a good solid horse. Good doer, I've always said. Sniff of hay and he keeps his weight on. Smart too. Ya can't fool him.'

Tiff didn't respond, simply adding she would be out later that morning to pick him up. Even though she wasn't looking forward to another long trip, she felt relieved, as though a tremendous burden had been lifted off her shoulders.

She decided that she would take a few buckets of feed to help entice Toby onto the float, as she didn't want a repeat of yesterday's fiasco.

Tiff and Col set off again, this time knowing what to expect and, as the miles disappeared behind them, Tiff was filled with a new kind of dread. What if he was too weak to survive the journey and stumbled and broke a leg? But in her mind, she could picture Toby rolling in the soft green grass just as Bundy had done the afternoon before.

When they arrived at the property it was even hotter than the day before. Within a few minutes, sweat was running down her face.

Col stayed in the car with the air conditioner running while Tiff went to find Gary.

The first thing she noticed was a truck at the side of the property. It had a rusty red crate on the back, a livestock crate. Her heart skipped a beat and her pace quickened. She could see Gary in the distance with another person, and as she approached she saw Toby. He was on the ground. It was obvious that he had stumbled and lacked the strength to get back up but this fact was lost on these two cretins, who were hitting him unmercifully.

By the time Tiff had made it to them, she was shouting at them to stop. They looked up, startled for a moment before exchanging a look of utter contempt. A hysterical woman. That was all they needed.

But Tiff wasn't about to be silenced or ignored. She demanded to know what was going on. The other man responded patronisingly, 'Look little lady, I'm here to pick him up. He can either get on the truck or I can hoist him on.' Not surprisingly, Gary's charm evaporated in the company of another male. He simply added indifferently, 'Sorry, he made it here first.'

Tiff looked from one man to the other and all she saw was defiant indifference. Predators who had no mercy. And then she looked at Toby. Poor sweet Toby, struggling to get to his feet. Attempting to do as he was told even in the face of such cruelty.

In that moment, Tiff felt the weight of the world crush down upon her. The sickening inequality of those who had power over those who were powerless. How one individual could 'own' another and deem them worthless and undeserving of compassion. The perilous situation those 'worthless' souls found themselves in, suffering and in pain. He had neither the strength nor the will to fight, even if it had been in his nature. Instead, he submitted with quiet acceptance.

Suddenly the arrogance drained from Gary's face. Tiff looked at him, unsure of what was happening. He leaned over and whispered something into the other man's ear and he too stopped hitting Toby and stood up.

'Take the worthless piece of shit, if he's that important to you,' he spat out at her and turned to leave.

But Tiff wasn't about to let them go just yet. She uttered five words: 'Help me get him up' and they complied.

With gentle pressure and encouragement, they managed to get Toby to his feet. The man then bid a hasty retreat and Tiff was relieved to see his truck speeding off down the road.

When Toby felt a gentle pull on the headstall, he resisted at first, too hot, too tired to move. But Tiff persisted, so he took a feeble step forwards and the pressure stopped. There was another pull, so he moved forwards again. They walked slowly and painfully around to the front of the property together.

Col got out of the car, not looking forward to loading Toby into the float, and Tiff told him what had just happened.

'I wonder what he said to him,' he replied.

'Probably just told him about our sex life,' Tiff said.

Col gave her a curious look and she added, 'You know, how I'm a Mountie.'

Col unhooked the ramp, opened the bar and waited. Tiffany gave Toby a handful of feed from the bucket and his ears pricked forwards.

When she offered him some more food, he relaxed. He took a mouthful and chewed. Tiff moved away, so he followed and ate from her outstretched hand. She moved again and he followed, step by step up the ramp into the small, enclosed space. He stood quietly as Tiff tied the lead rope and then gave him the whole bucket of feed.

Col and Tiff were astounded and waited for something to go wrong. Tiff moved the bar into place, then Col closed the ramp. Toby didn't move; he just stood there happily munching on his feed. Only when the bolts were secured and the ramp hoisted and in place did they let out their breath. Tiff entered the float through the side door with a bucket of water, which Toby refused. He was too interested in the feed to be bothered with anything else.

'It's almost as if he knows we're taking him away from all this,' Col muttered under his breath.

'I wouldn't doubt it in the slightest,' Tiff replied.

It was a totally different car trip home from the day before. They chatted all the way about the events of the past two days, stopping a few times to offer Toby water. On the third attempt, his ears shot forwards, as if in surprise as to why people were being so kind to him, and he drank. They set off again and didn't stop until they reached the farm.

Col pulled up outside the paddock next to Bundy. Tiff had decided that she'd keep them separate for a while as she intended to supplement Toby's feed until he was stronger. On his own, he would be able to eat in peace and not be chased from his food.

When the float was backed into the paddock and the gate was shut, they opened the ramp and Tiff gently backed Toby out of the float. He stood still and looked around as if breathing in all the beauty. Even after she had unbuckled his

30

headstall, he just stood there, then finally he took a few tentative, weak steps over to a waiting Bundy and they rubbed noses. Bundy squealed with excitement and began throwing his head in the air. Toby walked back to Tiff and Col and her mother, Ann, then noticed the softness beneath his feet and put his head down to investigate. He pulled a mouthful of grass and ate it slowly. He dropped to his knees as if to roll but he didn't have the strength. He just laid down his head and rested.

Toby was the first thing Tiffany thought of when she woke.

Last night they had left him still lying down. Although it was unusual, he didn't seem to be in pain, just exhausted, and nobody could blame him for that.

This morning Toby was still lying down but when he saw Tiffany, he grunted and heaved his body up into the sitting position. With a huge effort, he got up onto his gangly legs and stood there teetering, then took a few tentative steps in her direction.

Tiff smiled, realising the huge effort he had made to greet her, even though he had only known her a short time. Again, she was struck by his intelligence and sense of knowing.

She went and got him a small bucket of feed, which he happily accepted. She looked at him and thought about all the things that she needed to do: give lots of small, nutri-tious, easily digestible feeds; give him a worming and a bath; and get the farrier out—but that could all wait a few days. The poor old guy just needed rest and some peace. He seemed to feel safe here, which was good. It was funny how she thought of him as old, even though he was still a baby, and she realised how much she longed to see him healthy and strong. She knew that it was going to be a long road ahead and there would be setbacks. She wasn't even a hundred per cent sure that he would make it, but she was glad that they had gone back to get him. She had no regrets. Instead, her heart was full and she had an overwhelming sense that things were exactly how they were meant to be.

CHAPTER 4

Obsessed

The horse obsession began early, even before Tiff could remember. Her older sister Dani was the same. Their mum, Ann, was totally confused by both of them as she wasn't horsey, nor was their father or any other relative.

When she was about eight, Dani began asking for riding lessons, and then Tiff started as well. Eventually, in an attempt to stop the constant barrage, Ann made a deal. If they were still interested in horses when they turned ten, then they could have lessons.

Just after Dani's tenth birthday, her dream became a reality.

It was a Saturday morning and they had just arrived at Mosley Park for her first lesson. The riding instructor brought Jamie around in front of her. He was a Welsh cob and, like most riding school horses, a sensible and agreeable gelding. But, to Dani, he looked like a wild, unbroken stallion. The horses in her dreams and imagination were much smaller than this and they didn't flick their head or dance around. This horse looked angry, and she began to convince herself that he was plotting to kill her.

Dani backed away but her mother caught her and asked her what was wrong. She replied that maybe she would leave it for another day. Ann was dumbfounded. This was the last thing she expected. After years of obsession, harassment and pestering, her daughter was trying to back out of her first riding lesson. If Ann hadn't paid upfront, she would have been quite relieved but as it stood, she was about to lose a substantial amount of money. So, she tried persuading and cajoling, neither of which worked. She then changed tack and tried to be tough, but Dani would have none of that. Finally, with the help of the riding instructor and another worker, they forcibly placed her on the poor horse. All the while Dani was screaming like someone possessed.

Ann thought that surely once they got going, Dani would realise that it wasn't that bad and would relax, but it wasn't to be. She screamed the entire circuit of the round yard. On the second pass, she grabbed hold of one of the panels, which was higher than she was, and managed to pull herself off the horse. She then clambered up on top, out of reach of everyone. There she stayed despite numerous efforts to entice her down.

Tiff watched the entire spectacle with an open mouth. She couldn't believe what was happening. How could Dani do this after she had waited so long? It was her golden opportunity, and she was running away from everyone.

When Ann started telling Dani that 'she had better get back on that horse because she had paid for the lesson', Tiff suddenly realised that the golden opportunity was, in fact, hers.

She piped up, 'I'll ride the horse'—but no one was listening.

They were all focused on Dani. Tiff tried again but was met with silence. Tiff's mother, meanwhile, was consoling herself with the fact that at least she hadn't bought all the gear.

Eventually, Tiff started shouting. 'I'll do it. Let me.'

The problem was that, at six, she was four years younger than the agreed contract age. But Ann looked at her and thought, *At least I'll get my money's worth.*

Ann also secretly hoped that Tiff would have the same reaction when placed on the horse and then this whole thing could be put to bed. With Dani finally back on the ground, now that no one was trying to make her ride, she agreed that her younger sibling could take over the lesson and Tiff was hoisted aboard Jamie.

It was in that instant that Tiff knew she was exactly where she was meant to be. It was as though she had waited her whole life for this moment. She grabbed the reins with the utmost confidence and placed her feet securely in the hurriedly shortened stirrups. The riding instructor gave Tiff a few tips about how to sit and how to hold the reins and reassured her that she would have a firm hold of Jamie the whole time. Tiff wasn't worried. She was actually a little disappointed that she was going to be led around because she wanted to ride by herself. But it was better than nothing, so she sat there soaking it all in.

At the age of six, Tiff realised that dreams could come true if you want them badly enough.

Of course, that was it. Tiff was hooked and Ann knew it was futile to try to backtrack now and make her wait until she was ten for her next ride. It was all she thought and talked about.

The following Saturday they came back and had another lesson and then one again the following week. Tiff's seventh birthday soon came along and, of course, all she wanted was horse gear—jodhpurs, a helmet and riding boots. She wore them everywhere, even when she wasn't riding because it made her feel as if she was.

In her lessons, Tiff concentrated intensely, taking in every instruction, trying her hardest to master each of the steps that she knew would make her a rider. Ann wished that she would show the same dedication at school or even with jobs at home, for that matter.

Dani eventually overcame her fears and started to ride too, although never with the same level of confidence or bravado as Tiff.

For the next six years, this was Tiff's life. Every spare moment was spent at the riding school with the horses. Every waking moment was spent dreaming about them. Nothing else mattered, nothing even came close. She was obsessed.

CHAPTER 5

A setback

There was no gentle awakening, no tranquil transition from slumber to consciousness. Just an electrifying jolt and a voice inside her head that said 'Toby'. The bedroom was dark and, as Tiff reached an arm out from under the covers, she felt the early morning chill. The clock said 4.58. She knew there was no use trying to go back to sleep, so she just lay there for about an hour thinking about him.

The main thing on Tiff's mind was colic.

Colic in horses, like babies, is a general term that refers to abdominal pain. It is often due to an accumulation of gas, fluid or feed.

Tiff was concerned Toby would have no limits, that after being starved for so long, he would want to fill the void inside him, even if it meant gorging himself. It would be so easy for his stomach or intestine to become compacted with feed. Sometimes colic is minor, but it can turn from a slight irritation to a life-threatening condition in a very short space of time and is one of the major causes of premature death in horses.

Yesterday, his first full day at Jinki, Toby had grazed, probably for the first time in a year. After a couple of hours without even lifting his head, Tiff did the tough parenting thing and locked him in his stable. He didn't seem to mind. She let him out again for a little while in the afternoon.

Tiff ventured out of bed when the bedroom walls began dancing with shards of speckled light, waking Col as she fumbled around trying to find her jeans and boots. Mumbling an apology, she shut the bedroom door and set off to see Toby.

Toby didn't look great, but he was okay, and he let out a little sigh when he saw her. Tiff took Toby's big head in her hands and planted a kiss between his eyes. It struck her that he didn't smell right. That sweet, horsey smell of sweat and dust and grassy breath just wasn't there. Instead, he smelled stale and musty, like an old jumper left in a bottom drawer, sour and forgotten.

She opened the stable door fully, allowing him to go out into the paddock. He shuffled slowly and stiffly, only taking a few steps before dropping his head to pull out a mouthful of grass. He ate slowly, much slower than yesterday, which Tiff thought was a good sign. Maybe he wasn't going to be greedy after all.

Around eleven, she decided to put him away and wandered down to the paddock. He wasn't eating and seemed reluctant to move but she put that down to him not wanting to be locked up again. With a bit of pressure on his headstall he complied, and she thought no more about it until later that afternoon when she went back to let him out.

Those few hours had seen a marked change in Toby's health. He seemed tired and had a lot of trouble walking, as though he was in terrible pain. He stood with his head bowed, almost touching the ground.

Tiff looked over the half-door and paused momentarily. Her first instinct was to yell 'Toby' but she resisted. 'Don't overreact,' she told herself. 'Everything's okay.' But as the seconds ticked away it became clear that things were not okay. 'Hey baby,' she said cheerfully but there was no response.

'Toby,' she called as she opened the door wide.

No response, no interest in going out. No interest in eating. This was bad.

By now Tiff's voice was starting to increase in pitch, in volume, in fear and in pain. 'Toby,' she called again as she put her hand on his neck. He was covered in sweat.

40

She cursed herself. How could he have gotten colic? She had been so careful but obviously not careful enough.

Mary pulled the ear pieces out and hung her stethoscope around her neck. Normally cheerful and happy, she was unusually subdued. 'My guess is it's an infection,' she said.

'An infection—I thought it was colic,' Tiff said, doubly dismayed. Not only had she missed the symptoms but she'd also got the diagnosis wrong.

'No, it's not colic,' Mary responded. 'Have you noticed any cuts or wounds?'

'No, nothing,' Tiff said, wracking her brain.

The vet looked over Toby's skeletal frame, trying hard to conceal the emotions she could feel welling inside her. 'Where did you get him from?'

'I bought his brother, the one outside. He was in a paddock out the back, he was going to the doggers the day I saved him.'

'Might have been kinder to let him go,' Mary observed bleakly.

Tiff had had the same thought a couple of times but had pushed it to the back of her mind, especially after having seen Toby munching away happily yesterday afternoon. The last thing she wanted to do was make him suffer. He had suffered enough.

Tiff realised that she needed to make a decision. Should she let him go? One needle and he would quietly slip away. No more fighting. No more pain. As much as she hated to admit it, it seemed like the right thing to do. Hell, they didn't even know what they were fighting against. Where was his infection? Then suddenly a light went off. Gary had told her that he had gelded Bundy the day before. Surely, he hadn't done Toby too?

She voiced her suspicions. Mary put her hand between Toby's hind legs and the reaction was quick and potent. His hoof shot out and hit the stable wall.

'Well, at least we know what we're dealing with,' she commented. 'So, my question now is, do you want to treat it?'

Tiff recognised the underlying tone. She also knew what most people would say but she wasn't like most people. She was visceral; she relied on her gut and her gut told her to try.

'Treat him,' she said with an urgency that surprised even her.

Mary went to the car to get her supplies.

Tiff brought some more bales of straw into the stable to support Toby while he was sedated. He softly sank to the ground. Mary cleaned up the horrible mess of dried blood and pus and found, much to her surprise, that there was still one testicle intact. She removed it and put in a couple of small stitches.

'What sort of subhuman would bother castrating a horse that they were planning to send to the slaughterhouse anyway?' Tiff snarled under her breath.

Mary overheard her and shook her head in disbelief. 'Some people are just beyond comprehension,' she replied.

Tiff, lost in her anger, didn't even hear her, instead answering her own question, 'Someone who just wanted to inflict more pain.'

Before she left, Mary checked Bundy and thankfully he was okay. She told Tiff she would be back in a day to check Toby and give him another shot of antibiotics.

Tiff decided to spend the night in the stable with Toby. She brought down a sleeping bag, a few pillows and a small radio, which she put on low so as not to disturb Toby. It was to try to deter any mice or rats that might decide to come calling. She wasn't phobic about them but didn't welcome the thought of waking up to find one walking across her face. While she heard a few scurrying noises through the night, thankfully there was no physical contact. She slept fitfully, waking every few hours to check Toby. Despite his fever, he wouldn't drink, which worried her, but he was still conscious.

When dawn broke, Tiff decided to get a cup of coffee. The yard was lit with the glow of the kitchen light and as she entered, she found Col and Ann silently sipping their brews. They looked at her but didn't ask any questions.

It was obvious there was no good news. She poured herself a cup and joined the silent congregation.

A few odd jobs managed to distract her throughout the day, but her thoughts always returned to Toby. Mary arrived late afternoon to check on him and looked grave. By this stage Tiff was beside herself.

'Why isn't he improving? We caught it early.'

Mary shook her head and gently explained the severity of Toby's situation. Severely malnourished horses quickly run out of body fat and start to use muscle mass for energy. This can also include essential organs such as the heart, liver and kidneys. Eventually, the damage to these organs becomes catastrophic. On top of that he also had an infection. In most cases, if they are caught early (which it was) and treated with suitable antibiotics, a horse will mend quite quickly. However, Toby was not strong to start with. He was weak and frail. All of his energy was going into maintaining his vital bodily functions. Suddenly his body needed to divert energy that he didn't have into healing, and it was slow.

Mary checked his temperature, gave him another injection and tried to prepare Tiff for the inevitable. 'Let me know how he is in the morning and whether I need to come out. You've done the best you could, you know that, don't you? In fact, you've done more than anyone I know would have.'

Tiff nodded and thanked her for coming out, then returned her gaze to the sunken frame of Toby laying prone before her, labouring for breath. A character she had barely gotten to know but could somehow sense was special. A life force fading away before her eyes.

'Fuck you,' she swore silently at Gary. 'I could have saved him if you hadn't done this to him.'

Toby stayed weak and feverish but did drink some water that night.

Tiff bedded down in the stable again. Each time she woke, she was sure she would find him dead, but he stayed with her. She began to tell him all the wonderful things they would do if he survived, how he would have the best of everything. Even though she tried to speak with conviction, deep inside she knew she was kidding herself. It was hopeless. Eventually she fell asleep exhausted, propped up against a hay bale. She woke after a few hours, frozen in the same position, aching and stiff. As she slowly untangled herself, she felt strangely self-conscious, as if someone was watching her. She glanced up and found two equally weary brown eyes staring back at her. She crawled over to Toby and wrapped her arms around his scrawny neck. She wanted to hug and squeeze him but she didn't dare. He was like a brittle twig, fragile and frail, so she just held him and cried.

Then Tiff fetched the water bucket and Toby took a long drink. Cautiously optimistic, she grabbed the thermometer and took his temperature. It was coming down. She let out

a breath that she seemed to have been holding for the past
two days.

It was too early to celebrate but, as Tiff looked at Toby,
she finally got the feeling that he wasn't going anywhere.
After the life that he had led, he had proven that he was a
fighter and now, finally, he had a life worth fighting for.

CHAPTER 6

Tia

Tia was a teenager just like Tiff. And like Tiff she was headstrong, determined and stubborn.

Most of Tiff's early childhood was spent with the horses at Mosley Park, but after six blissful years, Tiff's world was turned upside down when the owners decided to sell the land for development. For a horse-crazy twelve-year-old, it was a bitter pill to swallow. Everything she loved—the horses, the routine, the other people—was going to be wrenched away from her.

For the next two years, Tiff's only contact with horses was if she could beg or borrow a ride. Most kids would have lost interest, especially as Tiff was becoming a teenager. But it became obvious that this was no passing phase. She mourned deeply. Horses were her freedom, her passion.

All this time, her father steadfastly refused to buy Tiff a horse. All he saw was a huge outlay of money and then considerable ongoing costs. They had had this argument many times and Tiff had to admit that he was right in that respect. What he didn't understand, though, was that the monetary costs were nothing in comparison to the benefits that a horse could bring. Ann, Tiff's mum, knew this. She had seen Tiff bypass many of the typical teenage pitfalls because of her obsession with horses, but her father could not be convinced.

So Tiff did what any headstrong, determined and stubborn teenage girl would do. She got a job and decided to buy her own horse. She realised that if she bought it with her own money and paid for its agistment then nobody could ever take it away from her. The ongoing costs were going to be considerable, so she knew this was not going to be a temporary job.

Tiff found a part-time job in a shoe shop in Warriewood Square. Every Thursday night, Saturday and some Sundays she worked to save money for her dream horse. Her commitment made her the model employee, and her friendly, open manner made her a hit with the customers. Even at that tender age, Tiff was able to relate to people. She loved to share stories and tell a yarn.

Tiff scrimped and saved for twelve months. It wasn't a lot, and it certainly wouldn't buy a show horse, but it would buy a cheap one and that was all she wanted.

As luck would have it, a friend of Ann's mentioned that she had a mare for sale. It was rather serendipitous as Ann knew nothing of horses and was the last person Tiff expected to know of a horse for sale. Tiff wasn't normally superstitious but she took it as a sign. So, the next Saturday morning, the three of them, Tiff, Ann and Rob, her dad, hired a horse float and set off to see the horse.

It was a few hours easy drive. Just enough for Tiff to contemplate the enormity of the moment. She couldn't believe that in a few hours, she would own a horse. She was already mentally riding her when they arrived at the property. Kim met them at the gate and began to chat to Ann, but Tiff wasn't interested in exchanging pleasantries and wished they would hurry up. After what seemed like an hour, Kim led them through a gate and down a laneway and there, in a paddock, was a bay mare.

She was roughly 14.2 hands (around the height Tiff was looking for). She appeared healthy, had good feet and was not nervous . . . so Tiff bought her.

Kim seemed surprised that Tiff didn't ride her, but she didn't say anything. Why would she? She had just sold the horse.

It took a while for it to sink in. Tiff owned a horse. She actually owned a horse. After eight years of longing, wishing and dreaming, this horse was hers. She learned that the mare's name was Tia Maria, which sounded very sophisticated, so she decided to keep it. They loaded Tia into the float and off they went.

Not far into their journey, Tiff started to feel nauseous. Copious amounts of saliva kept flooding her mouth. Her head started aching and a queasy feeling began to rise from the pit of her stomach. She mentioned it to her parents and Ann told her to face the front. 'Of course you're going to feel sick, staring out the back window. What are you doing?'

Tiff explained that she was watching Tia, in case she fell.

No matter how many times Ann told Tiff to face the front, or how sick she became, she couldn't move her eyes off the little bay mare they towed in the float behind.

Years later, whenever Tiff thought back to that day, she shuddered. Impulse buying at its worst. She hadn't even ridden Tia. In retrospect, she realised that she was so desperate she would have bought a three-legged donkey. So, she was incredibly lucky that while Tia wasn't 'as quiet as a lamb', she was at least rideable.

In fact, for a horse that was bought with no trial or vet check, Tia ended up being not too bad. She was only green-broken and uneducated and not particularly well mannered, but Tiff was pleased that she didn't seem to want to kill her. She had two main speeds: walk and gallop, which suited Tiff just fine. Before long they were roaming all over the district. Nothing seemed to faze Tia, and Tiff loved the freedom of finally being able to go wherever she wanted at whatever speed she wanted.

Tiff had a friend from school who also owned a horse and agisted it 8 kilometres away. They had a habit of meeting halfway, or sometimes Tiff would ride the entire 8 kilometres, go for a ride, then ride home. They rode so many kilometres together that Tia often wore through the front of her shoes; when the farrier arrived to replace them, he would be greeted by two separate bars down each side, still nailed in place with the front missing.

Tiff's friend was a member of Manly Warringah Pony Club and encouraged Tiff to join, so she did. Every second Sunday she rode to the pony club grounds and participated in all of the activities they offered. It was great to be around other horse-crazy kids and she was able to further her knowledge and abilities because of the low-cost lessons available.

One day, a Mounted Police Officer came along and gave a presentation about her job. As she was leaving, she asked the kids if they would like to visit the Mounted Police complex at Redfern and meet the horses. The decision was a unanimous 'yes' and, within a few weeks, they were all strolling down the aisles of the historic stable block, meeting the towering bay horses that formed the troop.

Tiff couldn't believe her eyes. She had never seen horses so well schooled and disciplined, and she wondered whether she would ever get the opportunity to ride a horse like these. She doubted it, but it was nice to dream.

CHAPTER 7

Sid and Jock

Sid had lived on Jinki for a number of years. He wasn't old, even though there were days he felt it. He'd lost track of his age years ago, but he figured he was about sixty. He had worked his way around the countryside as a stockman before he went to Vietnam and then, when he returned, had resumed his travels. But as the years went by it became harder to work in the hot sun all day and so he settled here in paradise. He had a veteran's pension that covered most of his needs and Ann let him keep the van on the property in return for some light maintenance work. He had a keen eye for horses and years of experience handling them.

Jock was his best friend. He was a Stockhorse-cross and had been with him since he was a gangly colt. Sid had broken him in, then used him to muster stock. They had even competed in campdrafting competitions when they were younger. Sid was the only rider Jock had ever known. Sid had never raised his voice in anger to him and always treated him with kindness and respect. It really was a partnership made in heaven.

Over the years, Sid and Jock had travelled thousands of kilometres around rural New South Wales. They had worked on properties and driven stock in times of drought. But these days, their rides tended to be down a well-worn track, through the bush and across the beach to the local pub where Sid would have a few quiet ales. He had hammered a peg into a shady tree where he tethered Jock while he knocked back 'a few'. Jock didn't seem to mind; he too was getting older and seemed to like the fact that life was slowing down. Everyone knew Jock and would wander over to say hello and give him a treat. The other good thing about these rides was that sometimes, on the way home, they would stop at the beach and Sid would remove his saddle and let him have a roll in the sand and a swim in the ocean. Jock loved the beach, he loved life. It was a great retirement.

Tiff saw Sid emerging from his caravan and walked over to catch up. He'd been away helping a neighbour with fencing and he and Jock had arrived home earlier that morning.

Tiff didn't get a chance to make conversation before Sid pointed to Bundy and asked, 'Whose horse is that?'

'Mine,' replied Tiff. 'I bought him a few days ago.'

'Mnn, well, let's go and have a look at him.'

They wandered down to Bundy's paddock and almost on cue, as though someone had flicked a switch, he turned on the charm. He trotted past the fence, then cantered up and down the paddock, twisting and turning, bucking and rearing, snorting and blowing.

Sid watched him for a few minutes, then delivered his verdict. 'He's a dickhead. You better watch him.'

'What do you recommend then?' Tiff said, bemused. She loved hearing Sid's thoughts on life.

'You could put him in with Jock for a few days. That'll bring him down a peg or two.'

'Sure,' said Tiff, totally in agreement.

She grabbed a headstall and caught Bundy and led him into Jock's paddock.

Bundy and Jock eyed each other for a few moments before Bundy sauntered over to him cockily. Jock didn't suffer fools gladly and gave Bundy a nip on the shoulder to bring him into line. Bundy sprinted off in surprise and Jock followed him, neck outstretched and ears back just to reinforce the message. Later when he returned, Bundy was submissive and compliant, dutifully acknowledging Jock as the leader. With their positions in order, the two horses would now happily coexist and Bundy would learn some important lessons for his future: that there were hierarchies in life and he wasn't necessarily at the top.

Sid and Tiff watched this interaction with satisfaction. It was always good to see an elder showing a young one the way. Tiff waited for a minute or so and then she said, 'So, there's another one in the barn.'

Sid looked at her, surprised not so much by the revelation of another new horse but by her manner. Tiff knew she was being unusually reticent. Sid followed her into the barn and stood while she opened the door to one of the boxes.

Sid glanced inside and then took a few steps. He rested his hand on the horse's shoulder and Toby turned to look at him. Sid ran his hand gently down Toby's neck and gazed briefly into his eyes before turning to Tiff. 'He's a good horse. You did well.'

Sid never remarked on his emaciated state. Sure, he noticed it, how could he not? But he was not interested in the reasons. Obviously, someone had starved the horse, but he was safe now and what Sid had seen in those eyes assured him that Toby was worth saving.

CHAPTER 8

The fugitive

Tiff and Sid retired to a bench near the caravan.

It was good for Tiff to talk to Sid. He was not just another horse person; he was her mentor. If there was anyone in this world who understood her connection with horses, it was Sid. The show that they had just witnessed with Bundy and Jock was not lost on her. She was Bundy—young, cocky and overconfident—and Sid was Jock. Seasoned and wise, guiding her, helping her to become the best horseperson she could be.

'Heard you got accepted into the Mounties,' he said.

'Yep, still trying to get my head around that,' she replied.

'Why? You've always loved horses. I'm surprised you didn't do it sooner.'

Tiff agreed. She had thought about it when she left school but instead drifted towards her other great love, children, and became a nanny for some very wealthy clients.

Those years were great—caring for two young children, living on Sydney's affluent North Shore, and holidaying in luxury with the family. On one trip to Aspen, Colorado, Tiff even had her own chalet paid for by her employers.

Tiff had sold Tia when she was seventeen as she had outgrown her. By this stage Tia was no longer a 'wild thing' but quite an educated mare who was eagerly bought by a young pony club girl. This was probably the start of Tiff's lifelong commitment to training horses. It felt good to have trained Tia and found her a great home.

Her next horse was a little part-Arab filly called Rani. She had bought her at about twelve months of age and esti-mated that she would mature to just over 15 hands. Her reason for buying her was purely cosmetic. She had always wanted a buckskin horse. These horses are a creamy yellow colour with a black mane, tail and legs. Tiff thought she was beautiful and being a part-Arab, she had a showy style and presence. Rani was the first horse Tiff had ever fully trained and she was smart, friendly and very forgiving. Tiff learned what worked and what didn't through kindness and trial and error. Before long Rani was a reliable riding pony. Unfortunately, she never grew as big as Tiff expected—she stopped growing at about 14.1 hands—so she was not an option for Tiff in the long term. Tiff decided to move her to Jinki for her mum to ride.

In 1995 Tiff set off with a school friend to backpack around Europe. She loved the freedom and the adventure. The spur-of-the-moment decisions of where to travel next, what to eat and what to see. The element of danger that comes with travelling so far from home.

At the end of eight months, Tiff's friend ran out of money and had to return to Australia, but Tiff wasn't ready to go home yet. She had a working visa for the UK and a lot of experience with children. She approached a nannying agency and before long picked up a short-term contract with a family about to leave London for an eight-week holiday in Oxfordshire. When they arrived at the holiday house, Tiff was stunned to find that it was actually a ten-bedroom manor house with a conservatory and magnificent gardens. Of course, there were stables and some horses, so she was in her element.

She couldn't believe her luck and spent the next two months living in luxury, giving riding lessons and hacking about the countryside. Australian nannies were, and still are, highly prized in England and the young children loved hearing stories about her life Down Under. They were great kids and she grew very attached to them.

When that contract ended, she signed another with a family near Herne Hill, just outside of London. It was common practice in those days for employers to take the passports of their employees who were under contract. Tiff had not thought too much about it when she first arrived at the house, and the family was so lovely that she had no worries or concerns about getting it back. But, as time wore on, she began to get more and more depressed.

She had been away from home for ten months and was starting to get homesick. Mobile phones were not common and there was no social media in those days. Talking to her family and friends in Australia was expensive and difficult as there was a time difference of nine hours. Winter had set in, and it was cold and dark. The short days, the lack of vitamin D and the aching homesickness began to play with her mind, and she started to feel more and more frantic and trapped.

Finally, one day in an act of desperation, she packed up her belongings, waited until the family had gone out, and then rifled through the study until she found her passport. She called a taxi to take her to Heathrow airport and then fled home like a fugitive on the run.

Ann was horrified when she heard what Tiff had done and made her write a letter to the family apologising for abandoning them mid-contract. Tiff felt terrible but at the same time had never been so happy to be home. Luckily the family was understanding and there were no hard feelings.

When Tiff returned to Australia, she started nannying again. Although she loved the new children, she began to feel a bit empty. She realised that this lifestyle would not continue to satisfy her indefinitely. She wanted a career and a family of her own.

In 1996 she visited the Sydney Royal Easter Show. She had been many times before, and Tiff didn't expect this visit to be any different.

The New South Wales Mounted Police Unit perform five 'musical rides' during the ten days of the show. By chance, Tiff's visit that day happened to coincide with one of these rides. The musical ride is a series of precision drill movements performed in time to music played by the New South Wales Police Band.

Tiff sat there transfixed. She was amazed at the extraordinary skill and discipline of both the horses and riders. She could appreciate the hundreds of hours of practice it took to achieve these incredible manoeuvres and make them look so effortless. And she could imagine the incredible bond between horse and rider.

Tiff remembered the pony club visit to the police stables all those years ago and the awe she felt. Back then the idea of becoming a Mounted Police Officer seemed impossible, but today it felt doable. She made her way to the police stand and spoke to some of the officers about joining the Force, in particular the Mounted Police Unit. She learned about the various requirements and discovered that, to be accepted as a Mountie, you needed to spend three years doing general police duties before you could transfer across.

Suddenly everything began to feel 'right'. Almost as if she had been meant to go to the show that day and watch the ride. Tiff had a strong feeling that life was giving her a signal and that she should take notice. For the next 24 hours, it was all she could think and talk about. But life was busy, and she had responsibilities with her job as a nanny and two young children who depended on her.

She had also bought, trained and sold a number of different horses since her return from England and was now the proud owner of Ben, an aged thoroughbred gelding. He was the first really well-schooled horse she had ever owned or ridden. He was gifted to her in 1997 by a friend who passed away. Ben had initially been agisted at a stunning stable complex at Ingleside but when he came into her care, she couldn't afford the fees. She moved him to another place that was clean and well run with good facilities, but affordable.

So between her work and horses she was incredibly busy and it would be another twelve months before she set the wheels in motion and applied for a position with the New South Wales Police Force.

CHAPTER 9

Chosen

It had now been a week since Toby's rescue. Each day saw him grow stronger and Tiff's anxiety lessen. It hadn't been much of a holiday so far—sleeping in a stable, worrying herself sick about Toby's health—but now that he was showing signs of improvement, the holiday that Tiff had planned gradually began to take shape again. She was finally feeling relaxed. Waking up with the sun streaming in the window and hearing the waves crashing on the beach only 500 metres away, it was hard not to.

The hardest decision she had to make was whether to ride down to the beach in the early morning, the late afternoon or both. Most days she opted for both. Even in the short time she had been here, the sun and surf had worked their magic. Her skin was tanned, her hair lighter and her mood brighter.

Of a morning Tiff would sit with her coffee on a camp chair next to Toby's paddock, watching him graze. The moment he saw her, he would venture over and stand staring back at her with his soft, gentle brown eyes. Ann laughed and told her that they were beginning to remind her of Sid and Jock. Col wondered out loud whether he should start feeling jealous.

Tiff had to agree with them. Even she was surprised at her actions. Despite being initially so excited about Bundy, he had since paled into the background. He was a magnificent horse and Tiff was truly thrilled with him, but it was Toby whom she thought of first thing each morning, Toby who was always on her mind.

It was hard to believe the difference in the two horses in just one week. Obviously, Toby still looked gaunt and frail, but she noticed an improvement. Tiff glanced over Jinki's rolling hills, carpeted in rich foliage and shaded by towering gums. They were so lucky it was summer with its unlimited bounty of lush green grass. It almost seemed to make the horses bloom before her eyes with health and wellbeing.

A few more weeks and she knew she wouldn't have to hide Toby away anymore. It wasn't shame that made her feel this way but a genuine fear that people might think she had done this to him. That she was his abuser, not his saviour.

She had already started addressing some long-overdue health concerns. She had given both horses a good-quality worming paste and would repeat it again in a month. Mark the farrier had paid a visit to start the long process of repairing their hooves. At least Bundy's hooves were just overgrown. Toby's looked as though they had never been touched. There were chunks missing and cracks traversed all the way up the hoof to the coronet band. That he stood patiently as Mark trimmed and filed each hoof was extraordinary given how little he had been handled; his nature was just one of trust and acceptance, just as Sid had known. He then walked stiffly back to his paddock. He had grown accustomed to his terrible hooves, and it would take him a while to stop compensating and start walking normally again.

It was about now that the 'invisible lead rope' appeared. Ann noticed it first. Tiff had walked into Toby's paddock to turn his feed bin upright when Toby began to follow her. When she stopped, he stopped. Ann called out to her to turn around and there, two steps behind and breathing down her neck, was Toby. She did a loop of the paddock, and he stayed just behind her. She started to weave, and he followed her. Finally, she stopped in awe. This horse, a horse she had only known for one week, was demonstrating liberty training principles (wearing no tack and following the directions of a handler). The difference here was that Tiff hadn't even tried to teach him. He was doing it totally of his own free will.

While Ann thought it amazing, Tiff was stunned.

'You should have seen him. He's just like a giant puppy dog,' Ann told her partner Errol and Col later that afternoon. 'It's like there's this invisible lead rope attached to him. He just does whatever Tiffy does.'

'Yeah, but Mum, the thing is he's not a dog. He's a horse and they don't do this. Well, they can, but it takes hours and hours of training and a really strong bond.'

Despite Tiff's comments, no one seemed surprised, and Col even joked that now he had more reason to be jealous.

Sid was sitting under the tree communing with Jock. Every now and again a spiral of smoke would rise up above his head and then dissipate in the gentle breeze. Tiff was usually too busy of an afternoon mixing feeds to go over for a chat. Sid was quite happy left alone with his thoughts, so she never felt obliged anyway. But today was different. She had something on her mind.

'Your boy's coming along well. I think he's going to surprise all of us.'

'What do you mean?' asked Tiff.

'Some horses are slow to recover, they're fragile, but he's strong. He's got a strong mind.'

Tiff hadn't thought of him as strong, quite the opposite,

but she had to admit after what he'd been through, the fact that he was still with them was a miracle.

'So, he follows me around, like a dog,' she stated matter of factly.

Sid looked at her. 'And . . .?'

'Don't you think that's unusual?'

'Not if you've been chosen,' Sid answered.

'Chosen?' Tiff repeated. 'I saved him.'

'So you think,' said Sid, leaving the comment hanging in the air like honey.

There was silence. She wasn't sure how to answer something she didn't understand. She had spent her whole life in the company of horses, yet she had never met a horse like Toby. She had never experienced the feelings she felt when she was around him.

'He's chosen you as his human, it's as simple as that. Some horses do it.'

'But I'm not keeping him—I can't,' Tiff argued.

'Just wait and see. The universe has its ways.' With that Sid took a long draw on his cigarette and looked over the valley towards the beach. 'It would be worth your while to keep him,' he added after a moment. 'You don't come across horses like him very often.'

'He is very sweet,' Tiff agreed.

'He's more than that. You know he'd do anything for you, don't you? He'd probably die for you.'

They sat there in silence. She didn't know what to say and Sid realised he'd said far too much. The sun sank and the yard became dark.

The conversation stayed in Tiff's mind for days. She still had as many questions as she had answers but at least now she knew she wasn't alone in her feeling that there was something special about Toby. Sid could see it too. But it wasn't a suspicion for Sid. It was a fact.

Tiff spent half an hour morning and night grooming Toby, but she was making slow progress. He didn't look much better for all her efforts, so finally she decided to wash him. She hosed him down and shampooed him, scrubbing away the months of dirt, dust and dead skin. Such was Toby's trust in Tiff, he accepted it all without a qualm: the new sounds, the new smells, even the feel of the stream of water from the hose. All he did was shift his weight from one hind leg to the other, even as his whole body quivered. When Tiff released him, he trotted away unsteadily, doing a round of the yard, throwing his head. Tiff stood there and smiled. When Toby finally pulled up, he stood for a moment, pawing at the ground, before dropping and rolling in sheer delight. The horse that stood up was different from the one who had stood there only five minutes before. Yes, he was cleaner but it was more than that.

He was alive . . . he was truly alive.

CHAPTER 10

Entering the Force

It was easy for Tiff to lose herself at Jinki. Time was irrelevant. There were no deadlines or schedules. The natural beauty was exquisite. The climate, idyllic.

But even in the midst of this holiday, she would remember every now and then that she had a life back in Sydney and that that life was about to undergo an enormous change. It was the second major change in her life in the past three years. The first had been when she applied to join the New South Wales Police Force back in 1997.

She remembered how nervous she felt when her application form had arrived in the mail. It was almost too fat to fit in the letterbox. Tiff had to pull it sideways to get it out. There were so many forms she almost gave up and put them back in the envelope but when she found the introductory letter and a checklist, it began to make sense.

There was an aptitude (or knowledge) test, a psycho-metric test, a typing test, a swimming test, a physical and a medical. She also needed to possess a first-aid certificate and every applicant needed a clean driving record.

Of all the prerequisites, it was the physical that worried her most. There was a range of requirements that she needed to satisfy but one in particular totally freaked her out. She needed to be able to climb over a six-foot (1.82-metre) flat-faced wall, at speed!

Tiff's first objective was to improve her level of overall fitness and core strength to meet the general parts of the physical. Day one, she bounded out of bed, training schedule clear in her mind and spirits high. Day twenty-one, after hitting the snooze button two or three times, she struggled out of bed, telling herself it would soon be over. But she still had to face her biggest fear: the wall.

Tiff found a wall that matched the criteria and began a regular routine of throwing herself against it, in the hope that she might find some sort of technique to get over it. But nothing happened (except for scraped knees and elbows). She realised that if she was going to be successful, she needed to get more lift in her take-off so that she wasn't just hitting it like a pancake and then sliding unceremoniously off. So, she started jumping and leaping about wherever she went.

Walking along the road, she would jump up to try to touch branches out of reach. At home it was the wooden architraves on top of the doorframes.

Finally, she managed to get her hands on the top of the wall but then lost her grip and slipped back down. She tried again and again until her hands hurt and then decided to call it quits for the day and attempt it fresh the next morning.

Miraculously the next day she managed to hold on and ended up dangling there, not quite sure of what to do next. Over the next couple of days, she broke through the pain barrier several times as she learned to lift her body weight up by her arms. Finally there she was sitting on top of the wall, elated. The wall . . . the damn wall was conquered and with it came the realisation she could soon be a member of the New South Wales Police Force.

Sure enough, in August 1997, with all her tests and exams passed, Tiff was accepted and began her training at the Police Academy at Goulburn.

Leaving Ben was not easy, but she told herself it would only be for six months and, being quite old, he would probably enjoy the rest anyway. She had no other horses for the moment, which was fortunate, so after she had organised a friend to care for Ben she started packing for Goulburn.

A few days later, she waved goodbye to her little share house and housemates and left Mona Vale ready to begin her new life and career.

It was fun that first afternoon, walking around getting acquainted with all the buildings, services and accommodation. But it was soon apparent this was no holiday. Tiff felt like a kid who'd set off for a school camp, then suddenly realised they'd arrived at an army boot camp. It really was another world.

When she opened her eyes on her first full day, the pre-dawn wind was howling and the room was dark, providing very little incentive to climb out of bed, stiffly made and smallish as it was. This scenario would be repeated daily over the next few months. By 7 a.m. the recruits were lined up, faces flushed, their breath emitting vapour every time they spoke.

After a few days Tiff was fully immersed in the intensive six-month program aimed at taking green recruits and introducing them to a variety of critical subjects such as law training and weapons training. There were also lectures covering relevant legislation and police powers, and topics such as communications, ethics and traffic control.

Physical training sessions were held once or twice a week. The classes usually involved push-ups, sit-ups and supported chin-ups, and they were encouraged to use the gym as much as possible in their spare time. There were also aerobic activities, such as short-distance runs of 3 to 6 kilometres, as well as interval training or the 'beep test'. It was a strange sensation to have steam rising from her forehead and sweat dripping down her back while the temperature hovered around 6 degrees. Some days Tiff arrived back at her room at 5 p.m., other days not until 9 p.m. As the weeks flew by, she realised that she was fitter than she'd ever been. It was easier to get up, easier to do the work-outs, and a general feeling of vitality permeated everything she did.

Tiff had never considered herself a social person. She thought back to those afternoons when all her friends would head to Mona Vale beach after school and she'd head to the paddock to see Tia instead. She'd joined them a couple of times, standing around awkwardly while trying not to appear awkward. These experiences had been excruciating and she avoided repeating them at all costs. What she didn't realise was that it was awkward for everyone. Even the kids who acted the coolest were self-conscious and anxious. Everyone was one stupid comment away from utter humiliation. It was a knife's edge.

When she arrived at the Academy, she told her classmates not to expect her to join in their get-togethers. She wasn't into that. But she wasn't a teenager anymore. At twenty-two she now had some life experience behind her and dozens of hilarious stories to tell. She also loved hearing other people's stories of what they had done in their lives and why they had applied.

It occurred to Tiff that although she had initially joined the Force to be part of the Mounted unit, she identified strongly with everything she was being taught. She was finally contributing something to her community and making it safe for people to live their lives and raise their families. She hated the strong preying on the weak. The undisciplined putting everyone else at risk. Now her life had purpose and she was looking forward to making her mark.

Halfway through the course, Tiff spent two weeks riding around in a squad car, observing officers in action. The world looked very different from the back seat, but she was glad to be there. It was safe and secure. All she had to do was watch and learn and ask a few stupid questions. She knew it wouldn't be long until she was sitting in the front, making life-and-death decisions, and she didn't feel ready.

If that wasn't bad enough, her future was now so mysterious. Tiff had no idea where she would be stationed. Whether she would have to move to the country and if she would have time for her horses. It was as if a pea-soup fog had descended on her life, blocking out all her bearings. She had to focus day to day and forget any long-term plans.

She coped by learning to trust. In life and herself.

Just as Tiff was starting to get used to her 'work experience' phase, it was over, and she found herself back at the Academy. She was now in the last half of her course and the training seriously ramped up. There were sessions on firearms, batons, handcuffing, weaponless control tactics, drills and public order training. Tiff felt completely and utterly terrified. She had never touched or held a gun before and here the trainers were, handing her one to fire at a target. She also was expected to learn how to subdue and handcuff burly and aggressive criminals. But, as tough as the training was, it was never boring, and she was glad that she had decided to apply.

At the end of her course, Tiff was presented with her uniform. It was a pivotal moment. Gazing at the vivid blue, the badge, the boots and the belt, she felt a surge of pride. She had surprised herself over these past six months and couldn't believe how much she had learned and grown. But she knew it wasn't a solo effort. There had been so many people who had carried her along and without their support and encouragement she may not have made it. Sitting on her bed, holding her new uniform, she vowed to return the favour to whoever might need some encouragement in the future.

CHAPTER 11

Col

In February 1998, under a crystal-clear blue sky, Tiff and her classmates were sworn in by the Police Commissioner at their Attestation Ceremony. She emerged a Probationary Constable and was stationed at North Sydney along with another new graduate, Cathy.

Tiff had half-expected to be sent to a remote country town for her first posting. But it was a nice surprise. It meant she didn't have to move from Mona Vale or find agistment for Ben. Plus she was secretly excited to be policing in the middle of the city, where the action was.

For the first eight weeks in her new role, Tiff concentrated on being a sponge. She watched all of her colleagues' actions and responses and absorbed everything they did.

She was paired with two senior officers in a two-part 'buddy system', with each block consisting of four weeks. Her buddy coached and supported her, and she was expected to do very little except learn and ask questions.

At the end of the eight weeks, Tiff was given a bit of responsibility and some small tasks. At first, they were fairly simple but then, as she became more confident, they increased in number and complexity. After a few months, most of her initial fear and trepidation had evaporated. She would still occasionally get nervous but that was normal.

About this time, she met Col.

One day she and Cathy were called to remove a man from the back of a taxi. Like most new recruits, Tiff was eager to prove herself and responded enthusiastically to the call-out.

Tiff glanced into the back of the taxi and realised that maybe this was not going to be as easy as she thought. The man seemed to fill the entire back seat. She put her head in to ask him what he was doing and was hit by a blast of alcohol fumes. The taxi driver was pointing to his watch, becoming increasingly impatient. 'Time is money' he seemed to be saying. Tiff wasn't really paying attention to him, instead trying to work out what they were going to do. The man was completely unconscious.

Tiff and Cathy did everything they could think of: shouting and screaming, shaking his arms, rolling him back and forth, yet he slept on. Cathy got her water bottle and tried pouring water on him. That did nothing. They then attempted to physically remove him—one pushing, the other pulling—but he didn't budge an inch.

Realising that it was fruitless, they called for backup and sat down to wait till it arrived. Tiff couldn't believe her bad luck: one of her first assignments and she had to call for assistance. She had hoped that she might be able to do something spectacular in her first few months and this was hardly what she had in mind.

Before long a car pulled up and Col emerged. He managed, with considerable effort, to extricate the sleeping drunk from the taxi and lay him down on the grass. He then turned to Tiff and Cathy and said, 'What was so hard about that?'

A few weeks later, Col asked Tiff out. She agreed, so he picked her up and they went to the movies. She was chatty and cheerful until they arrived at the cinema and he bought two tickets for *Saving Private Ryan*. She was a little taken aback. She had been expecting to see a romantic comedy or something similarly light-hearted, but she didn't think too much of it until she emerged three blood-soaked hours later, unable to speak. Col noticed her change in demeanour and assumed that she was just tired.

Tiff wondered whether she had made the right decision going out with this man but decided to give him the benefit of the doubt. The next weekend they went on another, more conventional date, and then she was smitten.

Their romance was slow to start but once they got to know each other, it steadily gained momentum.

Before long Tiff had introduced him to the great passion in her life—horses. Col was incredibly agreeable, that was one of the things she loved about him. When she offered to teach him to ride, he was keen. She couldn't believe her luck. She knew she would need to find a man who was into horses or at the very least would accept that she was into horses. She didn't expect to find someone who knew nothing about horses but was eager to learn.

Soon, they had moved in together, renting a house on some acres in Dural, north-west of Sydney.

One weekend, they packed a bag and headed to Jinki to spend some quality 'horse' time together. Tiff took Ben along as she thought he would be the perfect teacher for Col.

Perfect autumn weather greeted them, still warm enough to swim but with none of the scorching, burning heat of summer. She saddled up the two horses and headed to the beach. She naively imagined that Col would be a natural, just like in the movies, and they would be able to canter off into the sunset together. Sadly, reality didn't quite match her fantasy. Col fell off—a lot. Unfortunately for Col, although Ben was a schoolmaster, he was also a 17-hand Thoroughbred so it was a long way to fall, but at least it was on sand.

Tiff realised that she would probably have to teach him the basics and that would take time, but he persisted and that impressed her even more.

Eventually, Col managed to become a competent rider and even bought a few horses himself, but he never really managed to get attached to them because no sooner would he start to get to know a horse than Tiff would sell it on him. She didn't do it out of malice; it was just that she was used to starting horses, educating them and then moving them on. Col was okay with that as he had never really found his forever horse and didn't have the time to devote to one anyway. He also liked the fact that he was helping Tiff find horses good homes. It was a great partnership.

All in all, they had a lot in common. They liked keeping busy and were happiest when they had a major project to work on. Loving the outdoor life and horses, it made sense to buy their own property, so they began searching. Eventually, in 1999, they found a few acres at Maraylya and made an offer. It was a huge stepping stone in their relationship but neither of them had any second thoughts. Their offer was accepted and from that moment on, they had no spare time. Every hour apart from work, sleeping and caring for their horses was spent improving the paddocks and fencing, and building a shed to live in. Life was great and Tiff really felt as though she had found her soulmate. She never forgot her dream to enter the Mounted Police Unit, but life was busy, and it wasn't always at the front of her mind. She was just content to ride along on this crazy, unpredictable, satisfying voyage of life.

CHAPTER 12

A few quirks

Unlike most mornings, there was very little conversation this particular day. They all had a tennis hangover. For people who went to bed early and rose at the crack of dawn, sitting up watching the Australian Open was taking its toll. Agassi was sure to take the title, they all agreed, but they were split on the women's comp. Tiff and her mum thought Martina Hingis, while Errol thought Jennifer Capriati. Col had no idea.

'Can you fill the jug, Tiffy?' Ann asked.

She rose reluctantly and walked over to the sink. Out of the corner of her eye she saw a dark shape lurking to the side of the window. Her police instincts kicked in and she spun to face it, bracing herself at the same time. It took a few seconds to register that it was Toby, standing innocently looking in at them.

'Holy shit,' she said, recovering her breath.

'What?' said Col, looking up with alarm.

'It's Toby. Someone mustn't have shut the gate.'

'Well, you were the last one out there. No one else has gone in his paddock.'

'Maybe Sid,' said Tiff, then realising that it was even more unlikely for Sid to leave a gate open than her, added, 'Nah.'

Tiff wasn't particularly worried about Toby taking off. He had gotten out and simply come looking for her. He wasn't going anywhere, so she grabbed a banana and continued on with the conversation about who had let him out. As no one would own up and they still blamed her, she walked out the back door to take the fugitive back to his paddock.

Ann followed her out. She had a bit of a soft spot for Toby. They stood there shaking their heads as he surveyed them calmly from the garden bed, a few bushes flattened and his scrawny body framed by bright flowers.

'Do you think he's put on any weight?' asked Tiff.

'Are you kidding? You wouldn't even think he was the same horse. What's it been, three weeks?'

Tiff smiled and her heart swelled. She was too close to him to realistically assess things like this. She thought— hoped—he looked better, but she wasn't sure.

'So, what do you think you're doing?' she asked him with a laugh.

Toby responded by reaching out and slurping up the banana skin she held in her hand.

Tiff waited, thinking he would curl up his lips in disgust, but he looked at her expectantly, hoping for more. She walked in, grabbed another banana, peeled it and offered it to him. He took it, chewing it a few times before swallowing it. There was no expression. It was as though he had eaten an apple or a carrot.

What the hell? she thought. This was bizarre. Was it because he had been starved? Would he eat anything and everything that was put in front of him? Would he start to rummage through garbage bins? It was all too horrifying to contemplate then she realised that she still hadn't worked out how he had gotten out in the first place.

Tiff walked down the driveway and Toby followed her like an oversized Labrador. Sure enough, his paddock gate was wide open. She put him back inside, gave him a pat and walked back to the house.

Not ten minutes later, a shadow was cast across the kitchen window: the sun's rays were momentarily blocked, as if clouds had suddenly brewed without warning. Toby, not content with the damage he had inflicted on Ann's poor garden, was back, this time standing even closer to the window to get a better view of them.

Tiff now knew that Toby was a gate opener. It wasn't common but some horses did work out how to do it. She led him back to the paddock and waited outside the gate but he stood there meekly like a little lamb. She bid him farewell and wandered out of his sight. From her vantage point behind a few trees, she could clearly see him, and she waited for him to work his magic. He stood for a few minutes and then, unbelievably, appeared to stealthily check both directions before mouthing the catch on the gate. It took less than thirty seconds for him to remove the chain and then he nudged the gate open with his nose. As he made his way happily up the driveway, she stepped out in front of him and he halted, staring at her for a moment. Tiff could have sworn a fleeting expression of 'oh shit' crossed his face.

It was back to the paddock and this time a clip placed on the chain to secure it. Tiff felt terrible for spoiling his fun as she walked back to the house, but she told herself it just wasn't safe. What if he got out at night and wandered down the road? No, his little jaunts had to stop. He couldn't just go wandering wherever he wanted, whenever he wanted.

Over the next few days other quirky little personality traits began to show themselves and Tiff was intrigued. She had been around horses most of her life and some of what she saw was unusual. She had always thought that Toby was one of a kind, and now she was convinced.

He was also young for such idiosyncratic traits to appear, only eighteen months old and severely neglected for much of that time. Usually, a confident horse in good circumstances may exhibit some distinctive behaviour, but generally, a mistreated horse will only be concerned with one thing: food. Toby still was an enthusiastic eater, but this was not the sum of his personality, merely a part.

The strangest habit he possessed could only be described as hoovering. He would run his rubbery lips over her skin in a clear sign of affection. But Tiff found it unsettling, especially when he would do it to her neck. She knew one false move and those jaws and teeth could do serious damage, but he never did. As her trust increased, she began to marvel at his devotion and wonder whether she was worthy. It did occur to her that she spent hours each day grooming him, so maybe he was just returning the favour.

Toby also took delight in taking her hat off. Sometimes just a gentle nudge to send it flying, other times he would take it in his teeth and hold it up in the air out of her reach. Tiff loved nothing better than laughing and Toby definitely made her laugh.

As Tiff stood there thinking about all his quirks, she realised that the lines were certainly beginning to blur when it came to Toby. She knew he was a horse, an animal, but more and more she was starting to think of him as a friend. A funny, complex, devoted friend who each day revealed more and more of himself to her. She remembered what Sid had said: 'It would be worth your while to keep him. You don't come across horses like him very often.' Sid was a man of few words but when he did speak, it was always the truth.

CHAPTER 13

The assault

It started out as an ordinary day.

Tiff and her partner Paul had been driving around when they got a call about a disturbance at a city pub. They showed up to find a young guy, drunk and obnoxious. Not a great combination but fairly typical. They told him it was time to move on and he was surprisingly compliant, which was good. But they doubted that he would actually leave without some intervention, so they asked him where he lived and then told him they would drop him at the nearest train station. He willingly got into the back of the paddy wagon, thanking them sincerely in his slurred, drunken manner.

It was only a five-minute drive to the station, but those five minutes was all it took to turn an affable drunk into a raging lunatic. Somewhere on the journey a switch was flicked in his inebriated brain. Maybe he'd had a bad day, a bad month or bad year—or maybe there was no reason at all. Maybe he was just an angry person who liked to get drunk and beat people up.

They pulled up at the train station. Tiff jumped out and opened the door of the wagon when his fist hit her squarely in the face. She was caught totally off guard, staggering backwards before falling to the ground. He came after her, kicking her savagely in the ribs before leaning down and punching her again and again.

She realised that she needed to get herself together and all of her training came flooding back to her. She managed to sit up and defensively block his next few punches, but he had the height advantage and kicked her down again.

All this time Paul, her partner, sat in the car on his phone, unaware of what was happening only a few metres away. Eventually, he got out to see what was taking so long and sprang into action. Within a minute he had hauled the man off Tiff, handcuffed him and shoved him back into the wagon, and they were on their way back to the police station to have him charged.

It wasn't the first time Tiff had been injured. In the early days, she had been a passenger in a squad car that had been in a pursuit when they were T-boned at an intersection. It was the first time she had experienced airbags inflating and that had been a terrifying experience, just as much as the initial impact. But they had saved her from serious injury and for that she was thankful.

This time she wasn't so lucky, although it could have been a lot worse.

Tiff went over and over it in her mind, thinking about what she could have done differently. Could she have been better prepared? Maybe her fitness had slipped a little? Maybe she had been a little too casual and trusting? She had to admit, the event changed her attitude towards drunks forever. So many times after this, she saw the same behaviour. Once reprimanded, they often displayed congenial, almost contrite behaviour, but this was part of the show. It was always a show. Later they let their guard down and the nastiness and violence returned. She saw it time and time again in the assault and domestic violence cases she handled. If there was anything positive to come from the experience, it was that she could now identify with the victims she needed to support.

But, in the back of her mind, Tiff was acutely aware of how different the scenario would have been if she had been on a horse. Horses had always been her safety zone, both mentally and physically. This experience, and all of the emotions she felt, really cemented her decision to apply for a transfer to the Mounted Police Unit, which she did at the end of 1999.

As it was, Tiff knew she needed to have served three years of general duties before she would be accepted and she was now two years in. She would be placed on a waiting list if successful, so the timing was perfect. She spoke to the necessary people, filled in the required paperwork, passed the required tests then waited for the call.

That call was for the practical riding exam.

Back in 2000, the entry requirements to the Mounted Police were very demanding. They were able to select from the cream of the crop of riders and gaining a place in the Force was extremely competitive.

Things began to change in about 2010, as top riders became harder and harder to recruit. The stables are located in Redfern and most experienced riders lived well out of Sydney. As time went on, it became difficult to find people willing to tackle the commute and the early morning starts, so they started accepting applicants who, while keen, were not experienced riders. These days, recruits are given lessons and trained and coached on their riding.

But in 2000, applicants were still expected to pass a riding test that was incredibly demanding, even for experienced riders like Tiff. She was very nervous about the assessment as she knew it would test her skill and stamina. She cruised through the saddled parts of the test and satisfactorily passed the intermediate requirements but came to a screaming halt with one of the final tasks. This involved riding around in a circle with no reins and no saddle; in fact, the rider's hands could not touch any part of the horse. She was instructed that she could ride with her arms out or by her sides, whatever felt most comfortable. The horse was put through his paces until she was cantering around with no hands, simply using her legs and seat for balance and guidance. Tiff found this manageable until they introduced a jump, then she lost her balance and fell off. She picked herself up, remounted and tried it again but on the second attempt, the same thing happened. After a third unsuccessful attempt, her confidence was severely eroded, and she felt desperate and distressed. She was angry with herself and the test and could see her dream slipping away and there was nothing she could do about it. She was also physically sore from the numerous falls and felt that she simply could not get back on.

Her reviewer also sensed that Tiff was about to give up and gave her some much-needed encouragement. He told her that this was the last thing she needed to do. That she had passed everything else with flying colours and that surely it was worth one more try. Gritting her teeth, she remounted and made her final attempt. Sure, it wasn't the most graceful of landings, but she made it. She was in!

She thought back to her pony club days all those years ago, when her club had visited the stables. Even though she had dreamed about becoming a Mountie, she never really imagined that one day it would become a reality. She remembered thinking that she had been lucky enough to get Tia, and to think that she could ride horses for a living was simply expecting too much.

And here Tiff was now. One week to go and she would be a member of the oldest continuous mounted unit in the world, older than the London Mounted Police and the Royal Canadian Mounties.

Tiff laughed. This holiday had been meant to be a chance to recharge so she could start in her new role fresh and energised. Instead, here she was, the new owner of two unbroken horses, one of them half-dead, and she was now wondering why on earth she always made life so complicated.

CHAPTER 14

Someone

Tomorrow was D Day. Departure day, back to Sydney to start her new life.

Tiff and Col spent the afternoon packing, then she saddled Ben for a final ride on the beach. Two tiny dots moving slowly in the distance were the only other signs of life. Unusual for this time of year. The low tide meant an expanse of moist, firm sand for them to enjoy but they needed to plough their way through the porcelain white, powdery stuff to get there first.

They jogged for a bit, and she could feel Ben's anticipation. He was waiting for her to let him go. She held him back just long enough to make sure he was listening and then gently touched his sides. He transitioned into a smooth canter, moving effortlessly, one ear back listening to her, the other forward, finely tuned to where they were going. Then she moved her hands up his neck a little and shifted her weight. She could feel his response already, as subtle as her own movements. She touched his sides again and he exploded with a force that stole her breath. She didn't check him; it was his time now.

They flew, swallowing the beach, leaving a misty spray in their wake. Her thoughts, concerns and worries all evaporated. She could have been anywhere in the world, at any time in history. She clung to him as he thundered on, his heart primed, pumping blood to sinewy muscles. They were between worlds, her favourite place.

They slowed as the beach disappeared behind them, making way for jagged rock pools and the windswept peninsula that lay ahead.

He was blowing, not from exhaustion but exhilaration, and the expectation of another burst of freedom.

She walked him for a few minutes to catch her breath, feeling him like a loaded spring beneath her. He wasn't listening to her like before but that was okay. He had connected with hundreds of years of his Thoroughbred heritage and that was good for his heart and soul. She knew he needed the release as much as she did. She touched him with her heels again and he shot forwards, not with the same ferocity but still a savage power.

Toby was waiting for them as they trotted up the driveway. She let Ben wander over and they touched noses, Toby highly interested in the smell of the salt that coated both their bodies. Tiff heard the bin lid closing and looked up to see Ann staring at them.

'The old and the new,' she remarked.

Tiff smiled. The same thought had fleetingly crossed her mind, but she added, 'Yeah, but I'm not keeping Toby.' As the words left her lips, they sounded strange. Like she was forcing them out and they hung there with no place to go. Ann nodded and walked back to the house, rubbish bin in hand.

Tiff looked at Toby and patted Ben's neck. Even if she wasn't planning to keep Toby, there was one thing she knew: she would show Toby the same patience when she started him that Ben had always shown her.

When she adopted Ben in 1997, he was an accomplished showjumper, and it was one discipline that Tiff had never attempted. Before long the temptation became too great. She started doing some low-level training on him—just trot poles and a few low jumps, aiming at getting her seat correct and learning how to hold her hands and then release them.

The following year, Amber, a colleague from the Police Force, learned of her endeavours and encouraged Tiff to join her at a jumping competition at Scheyville on Sydney's north-western fringe. Tiff was reluctant but she went along thinking that it would be a small competition and a good experience for her in some beginner classes.

As she discovered when they arrived, it was actually run by the Sydney Showjumping Club and there were no beginner classes. She had no alternative but to enter at the lowest height, which was well above what she ever had jumped before. She was trying to convince herself that it wouldn't matter if she knocked a few poles when Amber excitedly told her that there was a police class and that she had been approached by two Mounted Police officers who needed two people to make up a team of four. Amber had agreed and had put Tiff's name down as well.

Tiff was horrified. A team competition was the last thing she wanted to be a part of. She was already terrified that she would stuff up her own round, which would be bad enough, but she didn't want to be responsible for ruining someone else's results.

But the others would not hear of it. Every time she tried to object they would reply with things like 'everything will be fine' and 'Amber said you've been riding all your life' and of course 'Ben is amazing, he could do this course in his sleep'.

Tiff had no doubt that Ben could handle the jumps but just looking at the height of them made her feel physically sick. She felt even sicker when she realised that the two women were both senior constables and renowned show-jumpers. But there was nothing she could do to get out of it, apart from pretending to fall and hurt her ankle, which did seriously cross her mind.

Finally, it was Tiff's turn. She trotted out into the ring, all the time thinking about how misleading she must look. Here she was on a beautiful, elegant horse, looking very much in control. Everyone would expect her to fly around the course taking each jump confidently and with ease. Instead, she was about to demolish the course.

Which is exactly what happened. She misjudged the striding; she threw herself over some jumps and got left behind on others. Poor Ben didn't know what was happening. He had never had a round like that and Tiff felt bad for him. But not as bad as when she saw the others' faces. They were stunned. All she could do was remind them that she had told them she was a beginner. In an attempt to lighten the mood, she added light-heartedly, 'Well, at least I didn't fall off' but no one laughed.

After that, Tiff stuck to jumping in the arena at the stables, but the competition had taught her a lot. She instinctively knew what she had done wrong and was determined to correct it. She decided that a lower height was going to be a great starting point, and that she would need to work on her technique.

Ben had always been patient with her, like a kindly old grandfather. He was aged when she got him, and he helped her to not only learn to jump but also appreciate older horses. They were so often discarded, even after years of devoted service to their owners, or passed over by people with more confidence than skill or experience. People who could have benefited from their wisdom but were too arrogant to even recognise it.

As Tiff sat astride Ben, musing on these thoughts, she suddenly realised that she would now be working with the two Mounted officers from that jumping competition. She sincerely hoped they didn't recognise her when she started with them in two days time.

All the horses had been fed and she had packed up Ben and Samson's gear ready to put in the float in the morning. She knocked on the caravan door and Sid answered, midway through cooking dinner. He beckoned her to come in and cleared away some magazines for her to sit down. There was only a mouthful of rum left in his glass so he swallowed it and refilled the glass as he spoke.

'Heading off tomorrow?'

'Yeah, not looking forward to the trip.'

'I don't blame you.'

'Sid, I was wondering whether you'd mind Toby and Bundy for me while I'm away?'

'Of course.'

'And can you keep an eye on Toby? He's much stronger but just if anything happens . . . you know.'

'Will do,' Sid said. 'But I don't think it will; I think he's well and truly turned the corner.'

Tiff smiled. 'I won't be back for a couple of months, but I'll bring rugs for them when I do.'

Sid nodded. 'Do you want to show me what you feed Toby?'

'But you're cooking dinner.'

'It's okay; I was going to have another couple of drinks before then anyway.'

They wandered out to the barn, and she showed Sid the feed. Toby stood watching intently, almost like he was the one getting the instructions. Tiff laughed and said, 'Do you think he knows we're talking about him?'

'Yeah, I think he does,' said Sid. 'He's probably never had anyone show interest in him before, poor bugger.'

Sid was right. Tiff thought for a moment what it must have been like to be Toby. For so long, his life had been mind-numbingly boring. Day in, day out, no change. No joy, just pain. The burning hunger, the flies, the unrelenting heat.

He never learnt anything, and he never received even a hint of kindness. Judged as ugly, unworthy, stupid. Made to pay for the crime of being 'less saleable' than his brother.

Now he was 'someone'. He mattered. He mattered to her.

CHAPTER

CHAPTER 15

Learning the ropes

Tiff jolted awake when the alarm went off. Col was already up but her body was out of sync after the month's holiday and the dreadful night's sleep she'd just endured. Instead of getting the rest she needed, she had run through endless scenarios of what might happen to Toby, whether she could manage to start two unbroken horses in the next eighteen months and what her new job would be like. The Mounties were a small, select group—a group with a proud history and a very defined way of doing things. Tiff had been involved with horses for her entire life, but would her views align with theirs? Would her style of riding be what they were looking for? It was dark and chilly as she climbed into the car and began the long drive to the Bourke Street police complex at Redfern.

Tiff wondered how she was going to go, meeting all the other officers. She wasn't shy but there was always something overwhelming about being the new kid on the block. There were thirty horses and riders in the unit, as well as nine grooms, although she knew she wouldn't meet them all today. Patrols were conducted in two shifts: a day shift and an evening shift. She knew she'd be paired with a senior officer for a while, probably on the day shift, and a roster would determine what horse she would ride on any given day.

Tiff's first day was pretty uneventful. Everyone was friendly and helpful, and she managed to digest the almost overwhelming amount of information she'd been given. The only uncomfortable moment was when one of the officers, Karen, looked at her and asked, 'Do I know you from somewhere?' Of course, it was one of her teammates from the jumping competition. Luckily Tiff was an expert at changing the subject.

The days turned into weeks, and Tiff gradually became accustomed to the travel and the routine. Some days she couldn't believe that she was actually sitting astride these incredible horses. It was like a dream, too good to be true, but then she would remind herself of the years of hard work she had put in to get to this point. A moment later she would think about all the people who put in extraordinary effort and were never rewarded. Her emotions continued to seesaw until she accepted that she was finally at a place in

103

her life where she wanted to be and was thankful. She was also thankful for Isaac.

Isaac was a schoolmaster, a term used to describe a horse who has been there, done that. Generally, schoolmasters are older horses who have been in the unit for many years and can be ridden by anyone. Isaac was a kindly, middle-aged Cleveland Bay with a club foot. This is a tendon flaw that causes the hoof to be very upright. It can occur before or after birth when the bones grow faster than the tendons. As the horse ages, it can suffer from lameness issues but luckily Isaac seemed to be okay.

Isaac took Tiff as a nervous, new recruit and cosseted her through all her 'firsts'. Her first few patrols; her first New Year's Eve; and her first riot.

During those few months, every time Tiff thought about the approaching New Year's Eve, an unpleasant feeling would start to rise from the pit of her stomach. She tried to stop thinking about it or consciously change her thoughts, but the fear refused to be quelled and would soon bubble back to the surface.

The Sydney New Year's Eve fireworks are justifiably world famous. Tiff was rostered on that night for both the 9 p.m. and midnight displays, and she could simply not imagine sitting on a horse with fireworks exploding around her. She never mentioned her fears to anyone as they all seemed quite blasé about it.

As a junior, Tiff knew she would be paired with an experienced officer and that did allay her fears but only slightly. As the day loomed, she found out she was riding with Griffo and was relieved. He always gave clear instructions and plenty of direction. Sometimes she didn't want instructions but New Year's Eve would not be one of those days. She would take all the help she could get.

Griffo and Tiff set off through the city and meandered down through the Botanic Garden to Mrs Macquarie's Chair. The atmosphere was electric, the public was light-hearted and jovial, and the horses were behaving beautifully. She began to forget her fears and live in the moment.

Every year there are new products, new fads. This particular year it was glowsticks, long cylindrical tubes that activate when bent and display a variety of luminescent colours. You could also buy clips that interlocked the individual sticks into a crazy assortment of shapes. People wore zany hats and sunglasses and some sprouted long tentacles from their bodies.

Surprisingly the horses seemed okay with all of this. Tiff was still focused on the fireworks and kept repeating the directions that Griffo had given her: 'Legs on . . . firm hold.' She nervously counted down the minutes to 9 p.m. and the first fireworks display.

Tiff was talking to Griffo when out of the corner of her eye she saw something colourful approach them. It was so close she couldn't even see what it was till it had passed them. At that moment Griffo's horse, Ras, who had been caught completely off guard, reared up and fell over backwards. Griffo, caught equally by surprise, scrambled clear as his horse came crashing down. Before Griffo could catch him, Ras leapt to his feet and took off at a gallop.

Tiff realised that the colourful object was a frisbee made out of glowsticks that someone had flung into the crowd. Poor Ras had never seen such a thing and reacted in the only way he knew—taking flight. Tiff was sitting astride Isaac counting her blessings that he had not reacted at all when she suddenly realised she needed to take care of her partner.

She looked down at him and started to say something but he was shouting at her, 'GET THE BLOODY HORSE!'

Those few seconds had given Ras a huge head start. By the time Tiff had collected her wits and set off in hot pursuit, he was galloping off in the distance. She dug her heels into Isaac, and they too disappeared down the road.

It was night; it was dark and Ras was a dark bay colour. He was galloping wildly through the crowded streets of Sydney. It was a recipe for disaster. All thoughts of the 9 p.m. fireworks were banished as Tiff tried to chart a clear path after the runaway. Nothing seemed to slow Ras down and people were jumping out of the way like in some B-grade action movie—but this was no movie. Isaac was gaining on him slightly, but Tiff wasn't clear on how she would slow him down. She remembered to radio the base and tell them that there was an officer down and a horse loose, and felt pretty pleased with herself for recalling her training and managing to do it at a full gallop. Then up ahead she saw a man manoeuvring some steel-mesh fencing. He was blocking off a street and Ras was heading straight for him.

With all her strength and might she started screaming at him to 'SHUT THE GATE' but was aware that every noise that came out of her mouth was disappearing behind her as she galloped along.

There was simply no way that she could project her voice forwards at this speed. Sure enough, Ras galloped through the gap in the fencing and as the man saw another horse approaching, he closed the gap.

Tiff and Isaac skidded to a halt, and she started yelling again, but this time to 'OPEN THE GATE!'

For what seemed like an eternity, they danced around, and then once the gap was open, they set off again at break-neck speed.

Up ahead, Tiff saw that Ras had run himself into a dead end. He had slowed before reaching it, finally some of the steam from the pressure cooker of anxiety within him released. He stood there like a tightly wound spring, ready to explode, but at least not moving on. There were a few surprised members of the public standing near him, wondering what on earth had happened and where this horse had come from.

Tiff started calling out to them as she approached, 'Grab the reins' but only got blank looks in response. She repeated herself then realised that the people probably had no idea what she was talking about or what reins were.

She changed her approach: 'Grab him! Catch him!'

Finally, a burly-looking man walked over to him, seized the dangling reins, and spoke to him soothingly. Tiff arrived at this moment and jumped off Isaac and took the reins. She thanked the man before checking Ras to see if he was hurt. There were no obvious injuries and she let out a sigh of relief. She radioed back to base to tell them that the horse had been caught and then waited, holding the two horses, not sure what to do next.

By this stage, there was quite a crowd assembled. It's not every day you see a Mounted Police horse without its rider and another one in hot pursuit. Then, almost like Moses parting the Red Sea, the crowd divided, and a golf cart appeared with a council worker and none other than Griffo. He stepped out of the cart with crop in hand and helmet tucked under his arm, looking like an English lord about to go for a jaunt around the countryside.

By the time the 9 p.m. fireworks took place and then the midnight display, Tiff was past caring, and Isaac barely seemed to notice them. She mused at how different expectations and reality can be. How, as much as you can prepare yourself for a situation, something totally unexpected can and often does occur.

In a way, Tiff was glad it had happened to her. She had been so completely focused on the fireworks that she realised her fear was feeding on fear. What had happened was actually worse than what she had imagined (although she thought it would be her on the ground, not her partner). But in the end, she had stepped up and handled the situation like a professional. It finally gave her the confidence that she could handle this job and anything it had to throw at her.

It was May 2002 and the Mounted unit was attending the May Day March in Central Sydney. They had been advised to gather on a side road and would be called upon if required. After waiting for a while, all of the riders dismounted to stretch their legs and give the horses a rest. They were all standing around casually chatting when an urgent radio request came through that the demonstration had escalated and they were needed to help break up the protesters.

It was Tiff's first demonstration but, unlike her first New Year's Eve, she was feeling okay. She knew they would either stay in a line or work in pairs, head to tail, to cut through the gathering. She had been trained to do loops, working to disperse the crowd. But she hadn't been prepared for all the gear.

Isaac wore protective headgear called a pacifier. It covered his head and had a steel plate running down the front to protect his face. There was also chain threaded inside the leather reins to prevent them being cut by protesters and Tiff from losing control. Tiff herself had a Kevlar bulletproof vest and a visor to protect her eyes. This was in addition to her usual equipment such as the gun and ammunition belts. She felt very much like the Michelin Man when she first mounted Isaac, as she was so restricted. But she managed okay with the help of a mounting block. It never entered her mind as she slipped off him in the side street that she may not be able to get back on.

Sure enough, when the call came through that they were required, Tiff realised her dilemma. All of the other officers had long legs and slightly shorter horses. She had short legs and a 17-hand horse. Added to that, the bulletproof vest was so big on her that it severely restricted her leg movement. As the other riders catapulted up onto their mounts and took off, she couldn't even raise her foot to the stirrup.

One by one, horse and rider disappeared and as they did, Isaac became more and more agitated. Sure, he was a schoolmaster, but even schoolies have their limit. He couldn't understand what Tiff was doing. He wanted to join his mates and started dancing around. This made it even harder for Tiff to mount and then he started frantically running around in circles, and she was totally beside herself.

She knew that they worked in pairs, and she knew her partner was on his own. It was all too much to cope with and she had no idea what she was going to do when she saw a familiar face wandering down the road. It was the Assistant Commissioner coming to see where she was.

'Do you want a leg up, Tiffy?' he asked.

She had never been so pleased to see someone in all her life and replied, 'God yes!'

He grabbed her leg and literally threw her up and nearly over the other side of the saddle. She was caught by surprise but managed to grab the saddle as she went sailing through the air. She quickly found her stirrups and set off to catch up to the others and find her place in the line-up. When she got there, it was absolute chaos. She had not been prepared for anything like this and it took her a few moments to adjust.

She finally found Griffo and settled in alongside him and started moving forwards in the line. Suddenly the two horses in front of them stumbled and there was a sickening thud as they and their riders hit the bitumen. Tiff saw it in slow motion and then felt Isaac lurch forwards. She had no idea what was happening and grabbed the reins at the last minute. He managed to correct himself, as did Griffo's horse, and Tiff and Griffo immediately pulled them up to avoid stepping on the two downed horses and riders in front of them.

The two horses were flailing around. Every time they tried to stand their legs would go out from under them. A protester had brought a bucket full of marbles and had scattered them in front of the horses. In terms of disrupting their efforts, it was certainly effective. But it was also potentially deadly. The riders held their horses still while the marbles were cleared away. Luckily the two horses who went down were uninjured and the riders remounted.

One of the officers who fell continued for the rest of the day but mentioned to Tiff that her shoulder 'was really sore'. After her shift, she sought medical attention and found that it was actually broken in three places. Twenty years later, she is still receiving treatment to try to repair the damage.

Later when Tiff thought about the day's events, she was struck by the fact that she really couldn't anticipate what would happen in her job. When she joined the Mounties, she somehow had thought her life would be more predictable, but she had been wrong. Days that she feared the worst worked out okay; other days, when she felt really in control, ended in turmoil.

It was also hard work and dangerous. But it was real. Tiff felt alive. And if there was one thing she didn't want in life, it was a repetitive, tedious existence.

CHAPTER 16

Growing up

Summer rolled into autumn. The grass stopped growing and the trees started to drop their colourful cargo. Everything began a period of dormancy. Even the two young horses slowed down in their growth and activity. As the weather started to cool off, their coats began to thicken. The insulating fuzz gave them a slightly comical appearance, as did the long, hairy feathers that sprouted around their feet. When it rained, they had dry shelters to go into and plenty of shady trees for when the weather was fine.

Feed was still abundant and they spent hours happily grazing in the sunny, autumn weather. Bundy stayed with Jock, but Toby was in a paddock by himself as he still needed supplementary feeding.

Tiff got out of the car and took a deep breath. It had been four months since she'd last seen him. Toby looked like a horse. A real horse!

Not the broken-down bag of bones she had first found. Not the skinny, scrawny colt she left behind. Toby had bloomed; his coat was thick and healthy, and his eyes were bright. She blinked away tears, confused by their sudden appearance, and walked into the paddock to greet him.

Tiff and Col had driven up that day, arriving in the late afternoon. Bundy wasn't the slightest bit interested in her, but Toby had come to the gate and called out in a whinny that showed his transition from adolescence to adulthood. It was deeper, more powerful and forceful.

Tiff stood and wrapped her arms around his neck, a neck that only a few months ago was lean and gaunt. Now she struggled to properly encircle it. She stood back and looked at him. Apart from the change in his physical appearance it was his demeanour that caught her off guard. When she left, he was like a baby, but he had grown up so much in this time. He stared back at her with knowing eyes, eyes that held great wisdom, and she began to see what Sid had seen all those months before.

What Tiff couldn't believe was that the hug she gave was given back. Toby pressed his awkwardly big head into her back and pressed her into him, and was reluctant to leave her side even when his food was set out. She sat with him to make sure he ate, then afterwards as he dozed. Reluctantly she left him, kissing his sweet face before going into the house to unpack and shower.

Tiff was up at dawn, pulling on her clothes and silently tiptoeing out of the house. There was so much to do and not much time. She had one week. She knew she was lucky to have that as she'd only been in her role for four months.

With the balmy days of summer behind them and chill of winter approaching, Tiff wanted to get the boys used to wearing rugs. She put headstalls on them and tied them up. She was pleased with how they gave in to the pressure and stood still. At this early stage of training, it was imperative that she didn't concede anything. Both horses needed to recognise her as the leader. They needed to respect her decisions and accept them.

In her eyes, there was nothing worse than a horse with terrible ground manners—those who walked over the top of you, who refused to tie up or wouldn't stand still. These things were important in all horses but doubly important in horses of Bundy and Toby's size. A bad temper or ill manner in a heavy horse was a lethal combination. If she was to successfully start them and turn them into safe riding horses with a loving future, they needed to be manageable. Unmanageable horses had dismal prospects and usually ended up in a kill pen.

Although it must have felt stiff and cumbersome, Bundy gradually became accustomed to his rug and before long, accepted it without question. Toby, however, seemed less than impressed. Even after a week, he was still resisting when Tiff attempted to put it on him. It was odd, as he was normally so compliant, and she was sure that when the weather turned cold, he would be thankful. But for now, it was a battle, and a battle she was determined to win.

The farrier paid a visit to tidy up their hooves and she wormed them again. Each day she spent time teaching them to lead, tie up and back up (or walk backwards). She also did some float training with Bundy, their disastrous first experience still fresh in her mind.

Tiff also caught up with Sid that first morning, but he was edgy and unsettled—he'd asked Col to pick up some smokes in town. She had trouble engaging him in conversation so she waited, knowing that it wouldn't be long till Col was back with his cigarettes. She wasn't sure how long he'd been without but, judging by his state, she figured it must have been a while. Once he had the pack, he lit one and took a number of deep drags and then settled back in his seat. The anguish left his face and his agitated tapping ceased. Then he began to fill her in on the last few months.

His affection for Toby was obvious. He recounted tales of his growing confidence and brilliance. 'He's smart, really smart,' he told Tiff more than once.

'Maybe you should keep him,' Tiff suggested, wondering why she hadn't thought of this before.

'But I've got Jock,' Sid replied, surprised, and then added, 'Anyway it's not me that he wants.'

If Sid was trying to make her feel guilty, he succeeded. It wasn't that Tiff didn't want Toby. She wanted him more than anything, but he deserved so much more than the little time she had to give him. She loved him so much that she knew she had to let him go.

This scenario was repeated several times over the next six months. Col and Tiff would make the trip north for a few days to check on Toby and Bundy and spend a little time with them. Each time the two horses who met them were larger and more magnificent, Bundy particularly, with his jet-black coat and impressive conformation. Toby was still magnificent in Tiff's eyes, especially considering where he had come from, although he would never compare physically to his flashy brother.

The horses got used to them coming and going, although Toby would always be a little wistful for a few days after Tiff left, Sid said. Then one morning a large horse truck lurched into the driveway and spluttered to a stop. Two men appeared from the cab. They spoke briefly with Ann, and Sid fetched a headstall and lead rope. He entered Bundy and Jock's paddock and caught Bundy without much trouble. The three of them loaded him onto the truck, surprisingly with only a small amount of fuss, closed the ramp and drove off.

Bundy was en route to Col and Tiffany's property at Maraylya on the outskirts of Sydney. Tiff had decided that it was time he started some light training. He was mature enough and had responded well to all the schooling that she had done with him so far. At two and a half years of age, it was the optimal time for him to be started under saddle.

Jock and Toby were distressed at Bundy's departure and galloped around their paddocks in agitation. Sid looked at them and realised that there was no reason to keep them in separate paddocks anymore. Toby had filled out and was probably fatter than Jock. He didn't need extra feed. Sid also thought it would be nice for Toby to have some company. He'd been on his own for so long.

Sid caught Jock and led him into Toby's paddock. The two horses sniffed each other, then Jock gave a squeal and lunged half-heartedly at Toby, who retreated in submission. Jock was setting the boundaries; if they were to live together, then Toby had to acknowledge him as the boss. But Toby was not interested in challenging Jock in the slightest and already acknowledged him as the older, more dominant horse. Within ten minutes they were grazing happily as if nothing had ever happened.

Over the years Tiff had owned, trained and sold many horses. Most of the time she preferred to work with unbroken horses like Bundy. They were a clean slate, with no 'mistakes' attached to them. She could gentle them with her own methods and take it easy, building trust and confidence along the way. It was a lot of work, but she could then be sure that the horse would not have any future problems.

Tiff had learned that horses don't just develop bad habits on their own. They are always a result of human interaction: what someone has taught them to do either consciously or unconsciously, and what they have been allowed to get away with.

Green-broken horses, as long as they had been started well, were also good to work with. These were horses who had been started (broken to bridle and saddle) but had not had the miles put into them that was needed to make them reliable riding horses. Tiff would take these horses and ride them every day, refining their skills and giving them basic education. Then an average, intermediate rider could take over and pursue whatever discipline they desired.

Equestrian disciplines are incredibly varied. Competitive riders compete in dressage (riding a series of different movements aimed to showcase the horse and rider's harmony and balance), showjumping, eventing (consisting of three disciplines—dressage, showjumping and cross-country jumping), campdrafting (cutting a steer from a mob and guiding

119

them through a series of pegs), polo, polocrosse, hacking or showing (like a beauty contest for horses where they are judged on their breed characteristics, conformation and appearance), sporting (and mounted games played on horseback) and endurance riding (where horse and rider compete together over a marked trail of various distances—20, 40 or 80 kilometres, or other distances—within a specific maximum allowed time).

The final type of horse that sometimes found its way to Tiff was the problem horse. She didn't shy away from these horses but, by the same token, she was wary. This was because in some cases the horses were so damaged that they were dangerous, and nothing could be done for them. It broke her heart to have to admit defeat with a horse but occasionally it happened.

Tiff could sometimes turn around the bad training and behavioural outcomes of poor riding habits, but it was a lot of work, and she could never be absolutely confident in the horse's future ability or temperament. Even if the horse was sold to a confident rider, she couldn't be sure that at a later date it might not be resold to someone less experienced.

By the time Tiff bought Toby and Bundy, she had a wealth of knowledge and experience in training. Although she did not have any qualifications, her training methods came from her years of experience. She used her intuition a lot and listened to her heart. Every horse was an individual and a method that would work for one horse would not necessarily work for another. She always spent a bit of time getting to know the horse, observing them and then just taking it slowly. She could speed up or slow down the lessons accordingly. Ben was an invaluable partner in many of these training sessions. He was a steady, calming influence on a young horse and also a quiet source of inspiration when a lesson didn't go so well.

It was interesting that, despite their common heritage, Bundy was far more highly strung than Toby. Everything excited him and he was far less trusting of people and their motives than his half-brother. This was interesting given the startlingly different situations they had lived in when she bought them. If anything, she would have expected Toby to be the more difficult one, but he seemed to be quite the peacemaker.

Bundy progressed well but he was definitely not a horse for someone who lacked experience. More than once, he tested Tiff's considerable skill and patience, but she persisted, confident in the belief that he would make a top eventing horse. He had the size, stamina and intelligence to master the disciplines required: dressage, showjumping and cross-country. But he was young and green and needed a lot of miles put on him. She rode him every day for at least an hour, usually more. She tried to vary the sessions to make them interesting and also increase his exposure to a wide variety of situations. Sometimes it would be in the arena, sometimes in the paddock, and when he had a little more experience, along the quiet country roads. She also floated him regularly to desensitise him to floats; if he was to become a competition horse, he would spend a lot of time travelling.

Finally, Tiff felt Bundy had reached a level she was happy with, and she began to relax. It had been a challenging time and, although she never felt like she couldn't handle him, he was a handful. But it had been good. Tiff didn't like to stand still with anything, even training horses. There was always something new to learn and she felt as though she had climbed a few steps with this experience. Most of all she was glad that she had started him. Someone else with little or no patience and harsh methods would have ruined him. He would have become yet another horse trapped in a downward spiral of being bought and sold to unsuitable owners, slowly getting worse until, through no fault of his own, he ended up in a kill pen.

CHAPTER 17

The wedding

Bundy's first official outing was a rather unusual one for a green horse. Col and Tiff decided to get married in November 2002, and Tiff planned to ride Bundy to the wedding ceremony on the beach at Jinki. She had always dreamed of riding a stunning black horse and Bundy fitted the bill perfectly. But the horse in her vision was always calm and dignified. A magnificent horse who carried her without even needing guidance. She thought with a laugh, maybe a more accurate dream would have been to ride a 'wild black horse' because that is exactly what she was expecting.

Organising a wedding far from home took quite a lot of planning. Guest accommodation needed to be booked, a reception venue chosen, and of course the two horses,

Bundy and Samson, whom Tiff and Col were going to ride, had to be transported up to the farm and settled before the event.

Tiff was determined that the wedding would be simple and economical. She had always been a no-fuss kind of person and she was not about to change her ways now. They had a mortgage and other financial responsibilities, and she thought it was crazy to waste money on one day, regardless of how special it was.

Tiff had a favourite saying: 'Guess how much I got this for?' She loved a bargain and was proud of her thrifty ways. Long before computers, there was the *Trading Post*, the classifieds and, of course, good old garage sales. With the advent of technology came eBay, Gumtree and Marketplace. She loved repurposing items—not just horses—and with a property, there was always a wide variety of things that were needed: fencing, feed and water containers, gates, water tanks and building materials for sheds and stables. The list was endless and provided infinite opportunities to browse and bargain hunt. Col was never worried because she bought really useful stuff. In fact, he was rather impressed by her abilities.

When planning for the wedding, Tiff decided that she was not going to actually mention the word 'wedding'. She had noticed in the past how the moment it was used, the price of the meal, flowers, whatever, seemed to triple.

She simply booked a restaurant and chose a set menu for forty guests. She ordered a bouquet of flowers from the local florist and bought a second-hand wedding dress to which she added her own individual touches.

Finally, everything was organised. All she needed to worry about was whether it would rain and if Bundy would behave himself. He had been broken in in only a few short months and it was a lot to ask of him. He was not the most relaxed horse even at the best of times, but she was confident that he would pull it off. At least it was Tiff riding him and not Col. If he did decide to play up, she felt confident that she could handle him. It might even turn the wedding ceremony into a theatrical spectacle.

Luckily the day dawned fair, and Bundy's mood seemed quite agreeable, so Tiff began to relax.

She was sure that it was going to be a beautiful, perfect day. She reflected over the past few months and smiled at the thought of their 'romantic' engagement.

Earlier in the year, she had been lucky enough to win a weekend getaway in Sydney at the Mercure Hotel.

They had been dating for three years and had even bought a property together. There was no question that Tiffany wanted to spend the rest of her life with Col. They also wanted children in the not-too-distant future, so she felt confident that he would use this opportunity to ask her to marry him.

They set off and Tiff was beyond excited. It was like a fairytale. There were so many opportunities—standing on the balcony overlooking the lights of Sydney, standing on top of the Sydney Harbour Bridge, enjoying a romantic candlelit dinner for two—but they all passed without the important question being raised. By the end of the weekend, she was totally deflated although she didn't want to admit her disappointment, even to herself. She couldn't believe how badly she had misread the situation. She had never been the romantic type, and this just confirmed to her why.

On Monday afternoon, she arrived home from work tired. She walked in the back door, put her bags down and started to make herself a vegemite sandwich. She was careful not to make too much noise as Col was working night shift and due to start in a few hours. But something have woken him as he walked out of the bedroom door in his undies and up to her standing by the kitchen bench.

He took her hand and without waiting for a response said, 'Will you marry me?'

Her first reaction was to hit him. How could he do this to her? How could he have wasted so many opportunities while in Sydney and then do it here, like this? But when she thought about it, she had to laugh. He had caught her off guard and it was certainly different. She was sure no one else would have an engagement story quite like hers.

The wedding went off without a hitch. The weather and the food were exquisite, and Bundy behaved himself impeccably. Nobody would have believed that he had only been broken a few short months ago. It probably did help that she had ridden him with a queen bedsheet tied around her waist for a few days before the wedding, to get him used to a train.

After the wedding, Tiff and Col stayed on at Jinki for a few weeks and Bundy enjoyed his time with the other horses and had some carefree rides to the beach. He was maturing nicely, and Tiff was very impressed. She was keen to see how Toby would react under saddle but decided to give him a little more time. She already had one horse in training; there was no way that she could manage the two of them.

As the days went by, she found Toby's reactions interesting. Even though he was unbroken and couldn't be ridden, he almost seemed jealous of the time she spent with Bundy. When they would ride out the gate together, he would gallop up and down the fence line—usually a sign that a horse is missing its friend—and call out to them, and then when they returned, basically ignore them.

She was aware that 'crazy animal people' sometimes attributed human characteristics to non-human animals and as a professional employed in a field that involved both humans and animals, she was careful to maintain a degree of impartiality.

But, in private, as a person who had spent the majority of her life around animals, it wasn't a crazy idea at all. She knew that animals shared many of the same emotions that humans do. Certainly happiness, fear, excitement and loneliness but also sadness, guilt, anger and, yes, jealousy. Dogs were notorious for being jealous; that wasn't even really open for debate—so why not a horse?

Eventually, it came time for Col and Tiff to return home. Reluctantly they loaded up the car and hooked up the horse float. They loaded Bundy into it as his training was still only at a low level. Tiff was keen to start doing some low-level competitions on him to further his education. And for a competition horse, especially in a discipline like eventing, that learning would be a lifelong thing. Bundy went on to fulfil Tiff's expectations by winning some prestigious competitions, and he placed in many introductory and pre-liminary events.

Time went by quickly. It rained almost constantly for a few months and, when the rain finally subsided, the world was a luminescent shade of green. The countryside was so green that it almost hurt your eyes. The paddocks were brimming with feed, in some places as high as your thigh. Toby and Jock ate so much that they looked as though they would burst out of their skins. Toby had grown in every direction and was almost unrecognisable as the horse that had arrived two years ago.

When Tiff arrived again for the summer, she knew he was ready.

CHAPTER 18

Starting Toby

Toby and Tiff had an audience.

She should have known he'd be there. Even though it was an early morning start for Sid, this was one occasion he didn't want to miss. He sat on a stump just outside the paddock and watched as she walked up to Toby.

He wasn't there to scrutinise or criticise; he was just genuinely interested. If he felt he could offer some advice, he would offer it freely, but Tiff knew she was under no obligation to take it. This wasn't his horse. Tiff also knew that he would tell her if he thought there was a better way to do something, and she would accept his advice gratefully. She had learned so much from him these past ten years and it was comforting to have him sitting on the sidelines, watching on.

Tiff opened the gate, caught Toby and fitted a bridle onto his head. She could tell he wasn't thrilled by the large, fat piece of metal she put in his mouth. He moved his tongue around and chewed at it, but it stayed there, refusing to budge. It would have felt strange and a bit uncomfortable, but it didn't hurt him, and he gradually got used to it. She was eager to move on to the next steps but just because he was coping well was no reason to rush him. After a while, she removed the bridle and gave him a treat.

The next day she repeated the exercise and fitted two long reins to the bridle and drew them out behind him. Toby turned to watch what she was doing, still chewing on his bit like he'd done the day before. She spoke gently to him, telling him to move on, then she gave the reins a shake. Toby took a few steps, then stopped. The reins flapped against him again, so he moved forwards. They did this a few more times, eventually doing a large circuit around the paddock. By the end of the lesson, Toby had mastered the art of not only moving off but also stopping.

Tiff continued long reining for the next couple of days, increasing the length of each session and the complexity of the tasks. Toby responded exceptionally well, showing no fear and even seeming to anticipate each exercise. She taught him to turn, to trot and to back up. On the fifth day, she carefully placed a saddle blanket on his back and hoisted the saddle into place. It fitted over his withers snugly and didn't bother him at all. She tightened up the girth, leaving plenty of room, then turned to look at him. He was studying her with an interested look and made no attempt to nip her, so she walked him on and completed a lap around the paddock. When they returned to the same spot, she tightened the girth a few holes and waited for him to object—but he didn't. All going well, she might get on him tomorrow. This was all moving along at an amazing speed, which was just as well as she was only here for a few more days.

Sure enough, the next morning she saddled him up and put one foot into the stirrup. She stood there for a moment to see what he would do. As usual, he did nothing, so she swung her leg over his back and sat down in the saddle.

Toby stretched his head around and looked at her. Before long he felt a rap on his sides, a bit like the long reins when they flapped, bidding him to move forwards. He looked unsure about what he felt, so Tiff rapped him on the side again.

This time he heard Tiffany telling him to walk on, so he moved forwards slowly and carefully. His movements were stiff and stilted—it must have felt strange to have someone on his back for the first time. Everything else was the same, the reins telling him which way to go and pulling backwards when she wanted him to stop. They walked around the yard with Tiff talking to him and encouraging him constantly. After a while, she climbed down and took off all his tack.

Toby (foreground) on the property where he and Bundy were born, near Grafton, NSW, in 1999.

Bundy (centre) and Toby (right), both less than six months old, 1999.

Toby at Jinki. Finally healthy and happy, in 2002.

Toby and Tiff ready for patrol at the Mounted Police Museum in Redfern, 2004.
Photo: NSW Mounted Police Facebook

New South Wales Police Attestation Parade in Goulburn, December 2016.
Photo: NSW Mounted Police Facebook

Toby and Tiff
ready for patrol
outside the historic
gates of the
Mounted Police
Unit, 2004. *Photo:*
NSW Mounted Police
Facebook

Before heading out for a Christmas patrol, 24 December 2015. *Photo: NSW Mounted Police Facebook*

Riot training at Randwick Racecourse. *Photo: NSW Mounted Police Facebook*

Having a rest before work. *Photo: NSW Mounted Police Facebook*

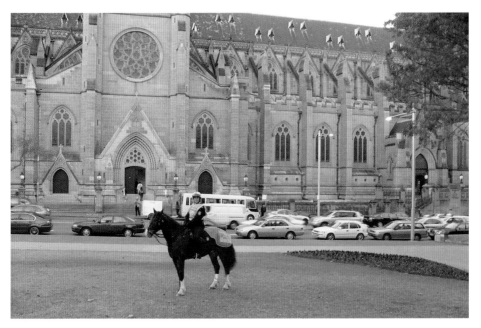

Toby and Tiff on patrol in Hyde Park, with St Mary's Cathedral in the background, 2004. *Photo: NSW Mounted Police Facebook*

Strutting out in the Best Presented Troop Horse event at the Sydney Royal Easter Show, 2016. *Photo: NSW Mounted Police Facebook*

Toby and Tiff getting ready for a high-visibility patrol of the Sydney CBD.
Photo: NSW Mounted Police Facebook

Taking a break from riding to admire himself in the mirror at the arena, May 2015. *Photo: NSW Mounted Police Facebook*

Tiff and Toby backstage, getting ready for the Military Tattoo with Brad Foster and Jack, 2010. *Photo: Courtesy Brad Foster*

The entire Mounted Police Unit posing in front of Government House, Sydney.
Photo: NSW Mounted Police Facebook

Patrolling the streets of
Redfern with Senior
Constable Kelly Dunn, 2004.
Photo: NSW Mounted Police Facebook

Toby showing off the prizes he won in the Troop Horse events at the Sydney Royal Easter Show—1st in team of four, 2nd in group of pairs, 2016. *Photo: NSW Mounted Police Facebook*

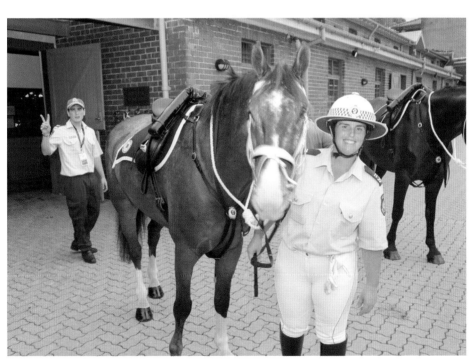

Toby and Tiff at the Mounted Police yards getting ready for the 2010 Military Tattoo. *Photo: NSW Mounted Police Facebook*

A grooming session with troop horse Jack. *Photo: NSW Mounted Police Facebook*

Toby's 'walk of shame' back to his stall after he was found to have let himself out. *Photo: NSW Mounted Police Facebook*

Toby celebrating Horses Birthday, traditionally observed in the southern hemisphere on 1 August.
Photo: NSW Mounted Police Facebook

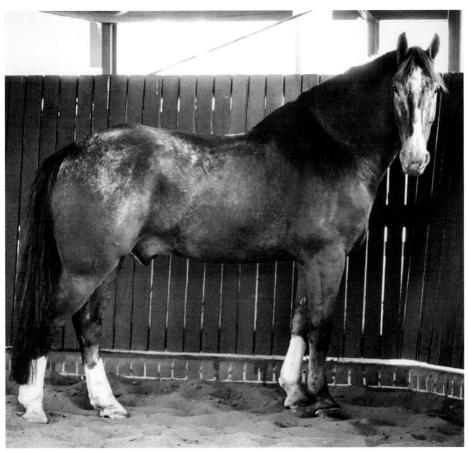

After a roll in the sand yard at work, 2015. *Photo: NSW Mounted Police Facebook*

Toby and Nadia Batten at the 100 years of Women in Policing celebrations out the front of Luna Park, Sydney, 2015. *Photo: NSW Mounted Police Facebook*

Toby, Nadia, Tony and Royal marking 100 years of Women in Policing, at Luna Park, 2015. *Photo: NSW Mounted Police Facebook*

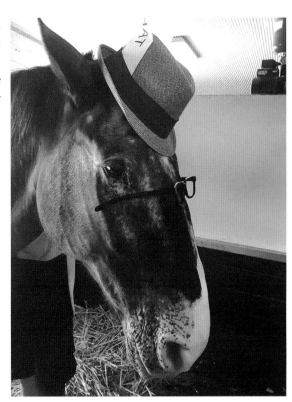

Dressing up at work
in the stables at the
Mounted Police complex.
*Photo: NSW Mounted Police
Facebook*

Toby and Nadia pose for a newspaper story about Toby being rescued and
becoming a Mounted Police horse, September 2015. *Photo: Steven Siewert,
Sydney Morning Herald*

Toby and Nadia at the rehearsal for the musical ride at the Royal Canberra Show.
Photo: NSW Mounted Police Facebook

Toby competing at the 2015 Sydney Royal Easter Show. *Photo: NSW Mounted Police Facebook*

Toby and Nadia at the White Ribbon Walk Against Family Violence at Coogee, November 2015. *Photo: NSW Mounted Police Facebook*

Toby (right) and Warrigal take time out to pose at the White Ribbon Walk, Coogee, November 2015. *Photo: NSW Mounted Police Facebook*

Toby with visitors to the Mounted Police stables at Redfern, 2013.
Photo: NSW Mounted Police Facebook

Toby (retired) and the Kurrajong Pony Club Team at a zone event at Megalong Valley, 2018.

Bundy, Diana (author), Tiff and Toby, 2023.
Photo: B. Williams/ A. Thurgood

The following days were the same. Toby stood patiently while Tiff saddled him, then she rode him around the round yard. She taught him to go from a walk to a trot, then back to a walk again. Toby took it all in his stride, but Tiff was astounded. This was undoubtedly the best horse she had ever started. He was so willing, so intelligent and so calm. While her weight and size were insignificant compared to his, he was acutely aware of her and he listened. It was almost like she was a small cog and he a large one, but they meshed together and worked as one.

Starting horses can be a dangerous activity. They are often scared and highly stressed trying to cope with new experiences and can be unpredictable. But Tiff never felt unsafe on Toby. At the end of the ten days, she felt even closer to him than before, if that was possible. She wholeheartedly believed that she could trust him with her life.

She was so in awe of him that now she didn't even notice the big plain head that had once stood out so prominently. In fact, most days she didn't even think of him as a horse. He was a delightful character, a wonderful companion and a beloved friend.

Toby had certainly captured her heart in a way that no other horse had, and she felt it tearing in two. She would have loved to keep him, but she just didn't have the time to devote to a horse like him. He was special and deserved to be the centre of someone's world. He obviously loved people, which was extraordinary given his early start to life. But he did and being left in a paddock for days at a time would simply be a waste of his intelligence and temperament. She and Sid had noticed he was already getting bored. She tried to imagine the person whom she was seeking to match up with him, but, for the first time in her life, she couldn't. His future was like a void. Tiff didn't worry. He could stay at the farm until something came up. There was no rush, and he was safe.

On their final day together, Tiff rode him down to the beach as a special treat. Col borrowed Jock and came with them, to provide some support to Toby.

Tiff couldn't wait to see his reaction when he saw the ocean for the first time. He stood at the edge of the track, where it opened out onto the beach, and gazed around him. He raised his head, flicked his ears forward and he even started pawing at the ground. She jumped down off him and removed his saddle, then walked down onto the beach. Toby only took a few steps before he hit the sand, rolling and kicking about, sending sand everywhere. He heaved himself to his feet with great effort and then couldn't resist having another roll. Tiffany stood there patiently, a wide smile on her face, and wondered what he would think of the water.

It was a very calm day, and the waves were only ankle-high, gently washing up on the shore before retreating like a bedsheet being pulled back across a mattress.

Toby took a bit of persuading before he put his front feet in the water and when a small wave washed over them, he was a bit startled. But Jock ploughed in boldly, so Toby followed. Tiff convinced him to move in further until the water lapped around his belly. He stood there for a while before he sat down like a dog with his bottom in the water and a self-satisfied look on his face. The sun was setting when they reluctantly dragged the horses away from the water, saddled them up, and rode home. Tiff too would have liked to stay and watch the moon rise over the water but there were things to do, and she had to leave tomorrow.

Tiff was anxious about leaving Toby. He had come so far in the past ten days; even though she knew that he wouldn't forget what he had learned, it would have been good if she could keep up the work. What he needed was some practice so it all became second nature to him. She went through different scenarios in her head, but nothing seemed plausible. They only had 2 hectares at Maraylya, and they already had three horses, Ben, Bundy and Samson, which put them at capacity. She was still working Bundy and didn't have time to train two while working full time. Toby would just have to wait until she came up again, but that wouldn't be for a few months. And then she would have to restart him with the basics, although the progress would be much quicker. She wished her mother lived a bit closer; six hours was such a long drive.

Tiff and Col unsaddled Toby and Jock and hosed them off. Sid was putting away the mower and a few tools and walked over for a chat.

'So how did the young fella like the beach?' he asked, patting Toby's neck.

'He's a water baby, for sure,' Tiff replied. 'I had to drag his sorry arse home. It's such a shame I have to leave tomorrow; he's come so far in ten days. I know he won't forget what he's learned but it would have been good to keep him going.'

Sid nodded thoughtfully for a moment and was silent, then said, 'Would you like me to put some miles on him?'

Tiff was amazed that she hadn't thought of this before. Sid was the perfect person to ride Toby; he was patient and kind, and an expert horseman—just what a green horse needed.

'Would you?' she asked.

'Of course. Jock might not be too impressed, but he'll cope. It would be good to train a young'un again,' he replied.

Tiff thanked him and went up into the house, feeling incredible relief.

It had been many years since Sid had been a stockman. Living here was great but it was pretty much the same, day in and day out. Although it had been a long time since he had worked a young horse, both he and Tiff knew he wouldn't have any problems. It was something that was in the blood and his blood ran thick with horses. He could instinctively feel what they felt. He could read signs too subtle for most people's eyes and he was acutely aware of the environment and anything that may cause stress or anxiety to his horse.

Apart from Tiff, there really was no better person to gently ease Toby into a lifetime partnership with humans. Sid realised the responsibility that he was about to undertake, and he took it with sincerity. This was a crucial time that could either make or break a young horse. Too much discipline and they would become either fearful or sour; too little and they may become dangerous.

Sid instinctively knew the balance, the fine line between coaxing and correction, between reassuring a horse and reprimanding it. A young horse that is ridden by a rider like Sid grows in confidence and self-assurance. It learns to trust.

For a horse like Toby, who had been so severely let down so early in life, it was a blessing. A chance to undo the disappointment and sadness. A chance to grow, a chance to shine. A true second chance.

CHAPTER 19

The tourist

Col and Tiff woke early the next morning. They packed the car and left just before 9 a.m. Toby saw them leave. It had happened enough times for him to know that life was about to return to its lazy, predictable routine. But this time, he was mistaken.

Around mid-morning, Sid arrived at his paddock. He didn't rise at the crack of dawn anymore. He had slowed down over the years and, although it disappointed him, he was realistic. He was getting old. There was the usual pain in his knees and back but some days there were random pains in other parts of his body. He didn't go to the doctor. He didn't think they could do anything anyway, except tell him to stop drinking and smoking, and neither of those things were possible.

After he had returned from Vietnam, the grog and smokes had kept him sane. They helped to numb the horrors that played over and over in his mind, and to quell the fears that had followed him home from the jungle. Fears he could not leave behind. Fear of darkness and of blinding lights, of loud noises and of silence. Fear of moving forwards and fear of staying put.

Sid came home to a world he didn't relate to and people who couldn't relate to him. He was twenty-one.

He sometimes wondered what his life would be like if his name hadn't been drawn but then he told himself that you can't live in a world full of could haves and maybes. It was what it was, and he was determined to make the best of it—and the best of it was horses.

Delicate, complex creatures who were deeper than most people. Sid would rather spend time with a horse understanding its joys and fears than hearing about someone's new car or house. People were fickle; they claimed to be your friend but then discarded you like a cigarette butt. Horses didn't. They were friends for life. He'd had a few dogs and they showed the same devotion, the same depth, but they always left him. Bitten by snakes at a young age and the heartbreak was too much to bear. Horses lived longer and were hardier. He hoped beyond hope that Jock would outlive him.

There was no counselling or therapy after the war or even in the years that followed. Sid had self-medicated for a

long time and was acutely aware that he was both physically
and emotionally dependent. But he was at peace. His ration-
ale was that he was too old, too set in his ways to change
now and he wasn't hurting anyone but himself.

He was a kind and gentle man, with old-fashioned
manners and morals. He was lean and wiry with a shock
of white hair usually covered by his hat. His skin had deep
creases and was a permanent shade of chocolate, thanks to
years of working in the sun. He wore King Gee shorts and
a shirt all year round. Occasionally in the dead of winter, he
would pull on a jumper. There were no schedules or dates
in Sid's world. He did some work in the morning, went to
the pub for lunch, then did a bit more work in the late afternoon. He was honest, hardworking and had a sharp sense
of humour.

Sid caught Toby and saddled him up. He left the headstall on under the bridle so that he could tie him up at their
destination. Then, with a considerable degree of difficulty,
he climbed aboard. Even at this young age, Toby had good
manners. He stood perfectly still as Sid pulled himself up
and lurched around before finally swinging one leg over
the saddle and placing it in the stirrup. Toby seemed per-
plexed at what was happening as only Tiff had ridden him
until this point, but he didn't freak out. He knew Sid well.
Sid had fed and cared for him for the past eighteen months
and had always been kind and encouraging in his actions.

Together they set off down the road. Toby had no idea where they were going but Sid sensed he was happy. He trotted calmly, seemingly barely noticing Sid's weight, as he was as light as a feather. But like any good rider, Sid expertly guided Toby with his hands, legs, seat and voice.

Poor Jock, however, seemed shocked. He had been left behind by Sid and this had never happened to him before. He galloped up and down the paddock and whinnied after them, calling until they were out of earshot. Eventually, he calmed down and waited. He knew exactly where they were going.

Sid and Toby headed down the road, through the bush and onto the beach. Toby was overjoyed at the feeling of the sand under his feet. Sid sensed he wanted to roll and swim like he had when he was with Tiff, but Sid pushed him on.

'Not yet my friend, maybe on the way back, if you behave yourself.'

Sid rode him down to the water's edge and along the wet sand for a few kilometres, then turned and headed back up across the dry sand. This was hard going but Toby ploughed on, thankful when they reached the track again. They trotted down this track, then Sid pulled him up as they stepped onto the road. The streets were wide and lined by huge old gnarly trees. There were only a few cars as it wasn't the holiday season and Sid signalled to the drivers to slow down, which they did. Toby eyed them as he walked past. He didn't understand what they were but was beginning to realise that they wouldn't hurt him. Eventually, they stopped at a building and Sid took Toby over to a trough and offered him some water. Then he took off his saddle, clipped a lead rope to the headstall, tied him up and gave him a pat. 'I won't be long, old mate—not on your first day anyway,' he said with a laugh.

Sid was a regular at the pub. His counter lunch was an institution and if he ever missed a day, the patrons would call Ann to see if he was sick. But, apart from his aches and pains, Sid was rarely sick, which was rather surprising as he lived on a diet of beer, cigarettes, fried eggs and steak. His friends at the pub were his family and they loved hearing his latest thoughts on the world and current events. He had bought himself a television a few years earlier and liked watching the news, although he complained bitterly that the world was going to the pits.

His friends noticed that Sid was a bit more animated that day than usual. There seemed to be something on his mind.

After his first beer, he said to them, 'So, I've got a new horse today.'

Everyone was stunned. For as long as they had known him, he had only ever ridden Jock. They all feared the worst, but he reassured them that Jock was perfectly fine. He explained that he was just putting a few miles on a lovely green horse belonging to Ann's daughter.

Everyone was intrigued and before long a crowd of people spilled out of the pub and onto the footpath. They walked over to where Toby was tied up and gave him a pat, but their comments were far from flattering.

'God, he's ugly' and 'Where the hell did you find him?' were some of the nicer ones.

Sid was unfazed and replied in his usual manner, 'Ahh, go to hell the lotta ya. He's a good horse—better than any of your old nags.'

But as much as Sid made out he didn't care, he was hurt. He had known Toby long enough to recognise what an exceptional horse he was. And in that time, Toby's physical appearance had ceased to register. He simply saw the wonderful horse inside and not the plain, ugly head that other people saw. Then he thought about it some more and realised he was being silly. They didn't know Toby and they had no idea how much he meant to Sid. He had never mentioned him before, so they had nothing to base their opinion on, other than his physical appearance. He went back inside and had a counter lunch and a few more beers and the afternoon resumed its pleasant normality.

Sid checked his watch and downed his last beer. He said goodbye to his friends and wandered outside. He tightened the saddle and climbed aboard with even more difficulty than before, and off they set. Toby must have noticed that Sid was much 'looser' than he had been on the ride over but that didn't worry him. Then Sid started singing. Toby had never heard anyone sing before. Sid sang out loud and when he couldn't remember the words, he hummed. If you looked closely, you might have even thought that Toby was moving in time to the music. It was a lovely trip home except they didn't stop at the beach. 'No, too much work to do today matey—maybe tomorrow.'

When they got back to the paddock, Jock was miffed. He wouldn't look at Sid and turned his back on him in disgust. Sid went over to him and patted him. 'Don't be like that you old goose, this young bloke just needs a bit of work. I'll take you tomorrow.'

And he did. From that day on, the two horses alternated taking Sid to the pub and they seemed to understand the arrangement. Sid wasn't surprised. He knew that animals often comprehend far more than we give them credit for.

These pub rides were wonderful learning experiences for Toby. He got used to riding through the bush, along the beach and on roads. He had to be patient and wait around for Sid who, depending on the company and the quality of the conversation, might be there for anywhere up to three hours. There were always people wandering past who gave Toby a pat and sometimes a carrot or piece of bread. Sid had even taught him to canter, and he loved stretching his legs along the beach. Depending upon how desperate Sid was to get to the pub, they might even break into a gallop.

Life was good for Toby: there was nothing to fear and only good people around him, a far cry from his early life.

The people at the pub still gave Sid a hard time about Toby but it was mostly all in jest. They were pleased that Sid had found something new to focus on. He was an exceptional horseman, and it was great for him to use his talents. It even seemed to give him a new lease on life.

One day, a few weeks later, Sid and Toby set off from the pub as usual. It was a hot, sultry afternoon and Sid thought he might give Toby a quick swim on the way home as a reward for his patience in standing in the heat. They made their way down the track and onto the sand and were probably halfway to the water when Sid noticed a man standing down at the water's edge, screaming.

Sid had had a couple more beers than normal that day to 'compensate' for the heat, so it took him a few moments to register what was happening. He sensed something was very wrong and spurred Toby into a gallop. They sent sand flying as they thundered across the beach and arrived at the man, who by this time had stopped screaming and was looking at them in shock. Then he started shouting. It was obvious to Sid that he was very distressed, but he couldn't understand a word the man was saying, and he severely regretted having that last beer.

Finally, the man started gesturing wildly out to the sea and making spluttering noises. Sid thought he had gone quite mad but then he saw something. A dark shape out beyond the waves, something bobbing up and down. It was a person, and they were in trouble. The beach was notorious for rips and, clearly, this man had gotten caught in one. Sid knew that it was only a matter of time before that head went under again and didn't come back up, so he decided to go in after him.

Toby got the shock of his life as Sid's boots crashed into his sides, and he lunged forwards into the water. He had had a few swims over the past few months but they were in the shallow water, never in the deep. Suddenly Sid was pushing him to go further than he had gone before, and he panicked. He tried to turn back but Sid wouldn't let him. Spurred on by Sid's legs and words, he waded out until he could no longer reach the bottom. He started swimming and still Sid kicked him. He swam on and on, with only his head poking out of the water, not sure of what they were doing or where they were going. The water's current was strong, and he could feel its pull. He just wanted to return to the shore but Sid had other ideas. By this stage, Sid was shouting at him, 'Come on, come on, keep going.' Although he had no idea what was happening, he was a smart horse. He must have sensed the urgency in Sid's voice, and he somehow knew that it was important. This was not just a leisurely swim; he needed to do as Sid wanted, without question. He trusted Sid like he trusted Tiff, so he kept swimming.

Suddenly Toby saw a person shouting and spluttering and fighting to stay afloat. Without any guidance from Sid, he fought against the current and swam over to them and waited as Sid grabbed the person by the arm. A wave broke nearby and the man was wrenched from Sid's grip. He disappeared in the foam for a few moments and then reappeared a few metres away. Toby saw the man before Sid and changed his direction instantly. Even in the panic and chaos, Sid was acutely aware of what Toby was doing. By this stage, he was simply a passenger. Toby was actively chasing the man in the surf. One more time they got close, and once again, the waves dragged the man away. Time was running out. Sid knew it and Toby seemed to sense it. They made one last-minute lunge for the man just before a wave hit and Sid managed to grab him by the arm. This time there was no way he was letting go, even if it dislocated his shoulder or the other man's. For a moment they were flung backwards by the surf and the man collided with Toby. Sid used this opportunity to swing him around and drag him behind him across the back of Toby's rump. Luckily the man responded and had the strength to sit up and grab Sid around the waist. Although his grip was crushing, it was the greatest feeling. Sid knew the man was not going to let go so he turned Toby's head for the shore. Toby swam like a fish, his head the only part of him protruding from the water. He ploughed through the waves and before long could feel the sand beneath his feet.

He stood up and took heaving steps through the sinking sand until he reached the shore. No sooner had they made it than the man on the beach started screaming again and grabbed the man off Toby's back.

Sid realised at this point that the person they had rescued was actually a woman. And the man who was screaming and had first alerted them was probably her partner.

The man hugged the woman, who clutched at him and started sobbing. Sid asked her whether she was all right and she nodded. She looked pale and sat down on the sand.

'I think she needs to go to the hospital, mate,' he told the man, who nodded.

He started talking to the woman but Sid couldn't understand a word they were saying. It had been a surreal experience, and this made it even more so. He started to feel uncomfortable, so he climbed aboard Toby once more and headed off. He had plenty to do that afternoon and his saddle would need a bloody good clean. Salt water was not good for leather.

The man started calling out to him as he rode away, and he turned back several times to wave. He was going to call an ambulance when he got to a phone, but he didn't think the man would understand him if he had tried to explain that, so he just kept going.

Sid got a few extra beers the next day at the pub but sadly Toby wasn't there to share in the limelight—it was Jock's day.

Word had spread about a man on a horse who had saved a German tourist from drowning and as one local put it, 'You don't have to be Einstein to work out who that was.'

Sid was embarrassed and only made one comment. 'Maybe the ugly horse isn't that bad after all.'

When Tiff heard the story, she was amazed. For any horse to do what Toby had done would be exceptional, but for a young horse, it was simply astounding.

She also knew she needed to seriously start thinking about finding him a home. She had been putting it off, always telling herself that he needed more time. But deep down she knew she was being selfish. It was her that needed more time.

Tiff was so glad they'd gone back that day and saved him. She had no way of knowing that this was not all Toby was going to achieve. In fact, it was only the beginning of a truly remarkable life.

PART 2

Saving Tiff

'A single act of kindness throws out roots in all directions, and the roots spring up and make new trees.'

Amelia Earhart

CHAPTER 20

The musical ride

The musical rides were one of the things Tiff enjoyed most about her job as a Mounted Policewoman. They were, quite simply, an adrenalin rush.

The logistics of coordinating sixteen horses and riders in a series of intricate movements, and the level of discipline required from all, was incredible. And when it was all over, the high lasted for hours.

It was the 2003 Sydney Royal Easter Show and Tiff and the other officers were warming up for their second musical ride. They had already performed one, two days earlier, and that had gone off without a hitch despite there being several new horses in the line-up. Tiff was riding Dandy Boy, a relatively new recruit. He was a Thoroughbred ex-racehorse, as were most of the Mounted Police horses. Thoroughbreds are powerful, intelligent, good-looking horses but they can be a bit unpredictable in the early stages of training, and Dandy Boy was no exception.

Tiff was now considered one of the more experienced riders and was given the younger horses on a regular basis. She noticed that Dandy Boy was a little more flighty than usual when she mounted, and so she kept a firm hold on him. He appeared to settle down after a while and began the rehearsal with no trouble. They cantered around in wide circles, and he was fine when they began to prepare for the first cross-over. This is where individuals or pairs of horses gallop in diagonal lines across the arena, narrowly missing each other by a few inches. The manoeuvre is then repeated by each of the horses in the troop. As Dandy Boy galloped through the cross-over, he was brushed lightly by another horse going in the opposite direction. This unexpected contact combined with his excited state caused him to explode into a series of violent bucks, each one gaining in force and momentum.

When a horse starts to buck, there are usually a few seconds for the rider to evaluate what is happening. Time seems to momentarily stand still and then everything occurs in slow motion. In this instance, Tiff knew she was in trouble. Dandy Boy was not just overexcited, he was having a total meltdown and there was no way that Tiff could get him to listen to her. Her 75 kilos meant nothing to a 600-kilo horse whose brain was in overdrive.

She sat fast for the first few bucks and tried to bring his head back up and under control, but he was fighting against her. By this stage, the other riders had abandoned the rehearsal and were holding their horses still, to try to create a calming environment, but it had no effect. Dandy Boy continued to buck and the jolting force on Tiff's neck and head was becoming unbearable. She could feel herself losing her seat and braced herself for what was about to happen. She didn't fall often but when you ride horses for a living, especially young, inexperienced ones, falls are par for the course. It was still a horrible feeling, to know that she was about to hit the ground, at speed and from a great height, and she closed her eyes involuntarily as she went sailing through the air.

It had been a hot, dry autumn with the sultry, summery days continuing right through until April. The monthly rainfall had been well below average and whatever rain did fall evaporated almost immediately because of the heat. The ground in the warm-up arena was rock hard, the soil compacted through a combination of dehydration and heavy traffic. Had there been even a hint of moisture in the ground it might have been more forgiving. As it was, it was like hitting a concrete slab. None of this occurred to Tiff until she hit. She had prepared herself for the impact but when it happened it was like her body had been slammed into a wall by a ten-tonne truck.

Every single bone and joint felt the blow. All of the air was forced out of her lungs by the impact. Then in slow motion, she felt her head move backwards and then whip forwards before her helmet hit the ground with a sickening thud. And in that split second between the impact and losing consciousness, she was acutely aware of one thing: the intense, terrifying thought that she was about to die. Although no sound escaped her mouth, in her mind she was screaming, 'No, no, no'.

Then blackness.

The other horses and riders had stopped long before she hit the ground. They watched in horror as the events unfolded then raced to her side as she lay unconscious. Someone checked her breathing and started telling her not to move. Of course, she wasn't moving anyway.

The other Mounted Police were shouting directions; someone caught her horse, and another phoned an ambulance. She still showed no signs of life except for shallow breathing, and they kept her where she was. The ambulance arrived not long after and checked her vital signs. The paramedics put her in a cervical collar and placed her on a board before taking her away to Westmead Hospital.

Tiff woke with no idea where she was or what had happened. She soon realised she was in a hospital and she was a patient and then guessed that she had had some kind of accident. Her head was throbbing, her neck was burning, her ribs pounding and every bone in her body seemed to hurt. It was a while before anybody noticed that she had woken up and so she lay there in confusion, too weak to attract anyone's attention. Finally, a nurse came in to check on her and summoned a doctor.

In a very businesslike fashion, he told her that she was incredibly lucky. She had a bad concussion and sprains but hadn't suffered any serious spinal injuries. He then added, 'I'd take this as a warning. A lot of people would be dead or looking at life in a wheelchair after a fall like that.'

It was a confronting thought and one Tiff really didn't want to contemplate, so she changed the subject and asked how long she'd been unconscious.

'Well, you've been here about three hours. I'll get one of the nurses to call your husband. He'll be relieved. He's just gone to get a coffee,' he replied, then left her alone.

It was a lot to take in. Tiff honestly could not remember anything about what had happened, but it was obvious that she'd had a fall, probably from a horse. The last thing she remembered was having dinner with Col on Sunday night. The whole of Monday was an absolute blank. The more she tried to think, the more confused she became.

A wave of anxiety gripped her, and her mind started racing from one 'what if?' scenario to another. What if she had been killed? What if she'd broken her neck? What if the doctor was wrong and there was something seriously wrong with her? She moved her arms and legs, fingers and toes. Although it hurt like hell, she could still do it. She tried to lift her head off the pillow, but a shooting pain caused her to abandon that idea. She did manage to turn her head sideways and so she felt calmer and less panic-stricken. Suddenly, she felt a wave of exhaustion wash over her and she drifted back to sleep again.

When she woke again sometime later, Col was sitting next to the bed. He was relieved that she'd finally woken after many hours. Tiff made him promise that he would talk to the doctor about her memory loss and find out when she could go home. She was eager to get out of the hospital as she thought then she might be able to escape the feelings of fear and dread that were plaguing her. Even as she lay there speaking to Col, she felt anxious and stressed and she didn't like it; she was normally so positive and confident. She asked him about what had happened, and he told her a highly abridged version in an attempt to downplay it.

When the doctor made his rounds the next morning, he told her she could go home.

She was glad, believing that once she left hospital the strange feelings she was experiencing would cease and everything would return to normal.

CHAPTER 21

At home

Tiff was wrong.

As she walked out of the hospital later that afternoon, everything seemed different, but when she looked around, everyone seemed to be continuing with their normal routine. Tiff was the only one for whom time had stood still.

When Tiff got home, she was a bit lost as to what to do. She wasn't strong enough to do anything strenuous, but reading and watching television were not her thing. She knew it would be a while before she went back to work, a fact she was secretly thankful for. Apart from the physical trauma she was vaguely aware that emotionally she wasn't coping particularly well. These last few days she found herself teary and sensitive.

For the first couple of nights, when Tiff went to bed, sleep eluded her. She lay there trying to remember what had happened. She thought that if she could remember something, anything, it might help ease her worry that she was losing her mind. She hated feeling like she had lost control. She hated the lost hours, the lost memories.

Eventually her memory returned and when Tiff remembered the fall, she immediately wished she hadn't. From that point on, she went over and over it in her mind, reliving every part of the accident in excruciating detail.

Up until this point, Tiff had wondered why the fall had affected her so badly. Sure, it had been serious, but she'd had worse. But now she knew. She remembered her last thought as her helmet hit the ground before the void consumed her, and it was terrifying.

Tiff had always been a risk-taker. Invincible. But she had come face to face with her own mortality. She remembered thinking that she was about to die. That everything about her, all that she had learned and all that she still had to learn, was over.

Tiff was also hit by the realisation that even though she had cheated death, she had also come within a whisker of being permanently incapacitated. She could be lying here a paraplegic or, worse, a quadriplegic, unable to move. Her whole life irrevocably changed at the age of twenty-eight. She tried to imagine how she would have coped but it was beyond her comprehension. She suddenly felt a surge of empathy for people who had not been as fortunate as her.

As the days wore on, Tiff became increasingly hesitant and fearful, all the time trying to present a normal, happy facade to the people who knew her. She had no idea what was wrong or what had happened to her once confident, easygoing nature. The thought of going back to work was just too much, so she repeatedly shut it out of her mind. Days dissolved into each other, becoming a never-ending blur of nothingness. She felt heavier, the air felt thicker, everything was an effort; it was as though she was trudging through thick snow.

In 2003 mental health issues, although acknowledged, were not given the same attention as today. It was always obvious when someone was struggling on the job, but people tended to handle it in their own way, usually seeking support from an understanding colleague. Tiff considered herself lucky that she and Col were able to support each other through harrowing events, but this time it was different. She couldn't put into words what she felt or the depth of emotion that weighed her down.

Tiff eventually realised that what she was suffering from was probably post-traumatic stress disorder. Even though she had survived the accident, the thoughts of dying still plagued her mind. Things that used to delight her suddenly seemed frivolous. It was as if someone had turned out the light and extinguished all warmth in her life. But she was convinced that she just needed time and that eventually these feelings would pass. It had only been a few days, after all.

Over the next couple of weeks, Tiff found herself thinking more and more about work. She couldn't imagine what it would be like to ride in the city again, surrounded by people, trucks, cars and planes, let alone perform another musical ride. She wondered whether she would ever be able to feel relaxed or safe on a horse and whether it would pick up on her anxiety. Deep down she was sure it would, and she knew it would make the horse fearful too. She never thought about talking to anyone, convinced she was the only person to experience such stupid fears.

Tiff was determined to regain her nerve. She had no alternative. Losing her nerve was a death knell to her career. But as she discovered, it wasn't that easy. Occasionally she would start to feel as though she was making progress but then the darkness would return and swallow her up again.

One night, in an attempt to make some conversation, Col asked whether she'd checked on Toby recently and she instantly felt guilty. She'd been so wrapped up in her own misery that she hadn't even considered him. She visualised his big face with those brown, docile eyes and smiled. It was the first time she had smiled in a week.

Col had lit the fire and its warm glow was starting to reach out into the corners of the room. The television was on but more as a background noise and the comforting smell of garlic heralded dinner. But none of this registered with Tiff.

Tiff wasn't fully present. She had finally escaped her purgatory and shut down all those intrusive thoughts. In her mind she was back at the farm, training Toby, riding him on the beach and at peace.

She rang Ann and found that Toby was doing really well. He was loving his pub rides and swims at the beach although the weather was finally starting to cool off. As Tiff hung up the phone, she wished she could see Toby, but her days were taken up with doctor and physio visits. It was a shame as she had a feeling that visiting Toby would help far more than any medical appointment. While she had Ben, Bundy and Samson, there was something special about Toby. She couldn't put it into words but if anyone was going to restore her faith in horses, it was him.

Then a ridiculous idea started to form in Tiff's mind. It started as a realisation that if she was going to ride in the Police Force again, she wanted to ride a horse she could trust. Most of the horses at that time were Thoroughbreds and while they were in training, they could be unpredictable. Clydesdale-crosses like Toby had marvellous temperaments. They were bred to work with people and they had amazing stamina. They were also intelligent and calm. But they lacked the showy appearance of the Thoroughbred as well as the speed and grace required for exercises such as the musical ride.

But try as she might to forget it, Tiffany's ridiculous idea would not go away. It was ridiculous because she wasn't just considering a Clydesdale-cross as her new horse but Toby. Toby with his big, plain ugly head, his roman nose and three, not four, white socks. She had no doubt that he could handle the training, the noise and his duties, but he would never look the part.

Tiff knew the criteria for a horse to be accepted into the New South Wales Mounted Police and they were incredibly strict. Toby would actually meet most of them. He was a gelding, although a few mares had been chosen in the past. He was bay in colour (they accepted bay, black or brown). He was of sound health and free of blemishes and would pass a thorough veterinary examination. He would also be a minimum of 15.3 hands or approximately 164 centimetres at the withers when he matured. She hadn't properly measured him but thought he would come close to that.

Tiff also knew he would pass the temperament test, which would be conducted during his three-month trial if he was selected. His ability to work as part of a team, maintain his calmness in stressful situations, and general trainability would be assessed.

The one criterion that he would fail miserably, however, was the cosmetic one: the stipulation that he possess good conformation and a fine intelligent head.

As unreasonable as it sounded, Tiff knew the reason for this requirement.

The Mounted Police Unit's duties are split between Operation and Protocol Engagements.

Operational duties include searching country and suburban areas for missing persons, cadavers, prison escapees, wanted persons and drug plantations. The unit also provides crowd and traffic control for public events and for demonstrations, protests and riots.

Protocol Engagements are ceremonial occasions such as Olympic ticker-tape parades, Anzac Day marches and police or state funerals. Mounted escorts are also provided to VIPs including the governor-general, state governor and members of the royal family on official visits. And, of course, there is the famed musical ride.

All of these events, by tradition, demand uniformity. People expect to see pomp and ceremony and, sadly for Toby, physical attractiveness and beauty.

He didn't and would never measure up. Tiff knew this but she just couldn't let the idea go. She went through a number of different scenarios (maybe they wouldn't notice his plain head) but always ended up back at the same impasse (they would; they most definitely would). Despite this she had a feeling that she should at least try.

She casually mentioned it to Col later that evening and waited for his reaction. He stared at her strangely for a few moments before exploding into laughter. She waited patiently for him to stop so she could put forward her arguments (he would be a great test run for her boss), but he wouldn't. Every time he started to calm down, the thought of Toby lined up on parade would set him off and he'd start laughing again. Eventually Tiff walked off in disgust.

Col followed her. 'Sorry, I didn't realise you were serious—you are serious, aren't you?' he said.

'Of course I am,' she replied.

Col exploded into laughter again and added, 'I think that head injury was more serious than we thought.'

Tiff realised that she would need to sell her boss, Don, on the idea of Toby before she showed him a photo. She wondered whether she had one that presented Toby's head in a flattering light, but unfortunately his nose was the dominant feature in the few that she had. She picked the least egregious one, then wrote a glowing list of Toby's qualities and attributes (to make up for any shortcomings in the looks department).

She knew Don was a practical man who would at least listen to what she had to say. He was also experienced enough to realise that Thoroughbreds were not always the best choice for the job and that the rider's safety was the most important consideration.

Tiff could think about little else and planned what she wanted to say in the most minute detail, so that she would be prepared when she met Don in a few days. She would only have one chance and she didn't want to blow it.

There was so much riding on it. Her memories of the accident still haunted her, and she had no idea if she could go back and ride the other horses again. She had tried to imagine it but it was just blank—all she could see was Toby.

CHAPTER 22

History

Tiff was a little concerned. She knew Toby was a Clydesdale-cross Stockhorse. That's what Bundy had been advertised as, and Toby was his half-brother. But it sounded too common for the Mounted Police. Most of the horses that were accepted on a trial basis had detailed pedigrees and elegant-sounding names. There had been the odd Clydesdale-cross before but never with a Stockhorse and there had never been a Toby.

Tiff knew that Toby and Bundy had come from near Grafton and she often wished she'd asked Gary whom he'd bought them from, as the more she got to know this horse, the more he intrigued her. She was also interested to find out why Toby and Bundy were half-brothers and exactly the same age. Did someone purposely set out to breed them and if so, why?

The answer came to her unexpectedly, perhaps even serendipitously.

A few days after Tiff began questioning where Toby had come from, she was introduced to a woman who had bought a horse from the mid-North Coast around the same time as she had bought Toby and Bundy. Not only that but this woman's horse was also a Clydesdale–Stockhorse mix and exactly the same age. It seemed a remarkable coincidence and Tiff was intrigued. Luckily the woman still had the phone number of the breeder, so later that afternoon Tiff contacted him.

Tiff had no qualms about calling a complete stranger and after only a few minutes, she and Ken were chatting like old friends. Sharing a love of horses was always a great icebreaker but she soon found they had something else in common.

Ken confirmed that he had indeed bred Toby and Bundy and was shocked to learn of Toby's condition when Tiff bought him. He was horrified when he found out that she had literally saved him from slaughter by mere minutes.

Ken recalled that Toby had been 'a delightful foal', as was Bundy, and he believed that they had gone to a kind and loving home. He said that Gary appeared to be a caring and experienced horseman but that was clearly a front.

Tiff remembered what Gary had said about selling the property and working in the mines. She mentioned this to Ken and said she sincerely hoped he would never own animals again.

Ken agreed then went off the line momentarily to make another cup of tea. When he returned, he began to tell the story of Toby and Bundy, and what a story it was . . .

'So, it was a few years ago now, 1998, I suppose. There was a horse auction in town and I thought it might be worth a look. I wasn't really expecting to buy anything, but the prices were good, really good,' he added enthusiastically.

Tiff could easily relate to this and told him so, describing a few horses she'd bought on the spur of the moment, including Toby and Bundy.

Ken laughed then continued, 'So I'm walking along, and I come across a pen with six Stockhorse fillies and a Clydesdale colt. Gorgeous young horses, eighteen months old at best. Next thing you know I've bought the lot of them. I mainly wanted the colt, but the fillies were an added bonus. I organised for them to get trucked home and I get there just before them. I'm standing there looking at the paddock and trying to work out what I'm gonna do with the colt when I say to myself, "He's young, they're all young. I'll just leave them together for a few weeks while I build a stallion yard. Nothing's gonna happen."

'So obviously something did happen. Six times over,' he said with a laugh.

Tiff was amazed. 'No way! They wouldn't have been sexually mature. Female horses are usually two before they first cycle.'

'I know,' said Ken, 'and it was also the dead of winter. Temperatures not much above zero.

'Anyway, eleven months later I'm the proud owner of six little Clydesdale-cross foals, two of which of course are your boys.'

This was more than extraordinary; it was almost a scientific impossibility. Horses never breed in winter—the lengthening days of spring are what triggers their oestrus. Tiff had never heard of it before but when she counted back Toby's age, sure enough, it was right. Considering both the season and their sexual immaturity, she also would have thought it safe to leave the seven of them together for a few weeks. Also, Ken had no reason to lie about it.

'I sold them all when they were weaned, 'cause I had enough horses on my hands already and the drought was really starting to kick in. But if I'd known about him, I never would have . . .' his voice trailed off in despair.

'Yes, but he's okay now, they both are,' Tiff responded, trying to ease his burden. He was a lovely man and none of this was his fault.

He chatted for another twenty minutes, telling her about Toby's and Bundy's mothers. Toby's mum, White-eye, was a bay and Bundy's mum was a strawberry roan. They marvelled at the role genetics play in colour selection, then just before they hung up, Ken promised to send her some photos of the boys as foals.

When Tiff put the phone down, she felt strange. She had contacted Ken to try to find out where Toby had come from and now, even though she had the answers, she had even more questions. She had a feeling that she would never truly understand Toby, that there would always be an element of mystery about him.

Here he was, a horse about to apply to the New South Wales Mounted Police Force. A horse who had overcome so much adversity in his life to reach this point. A horse who by the laws of science and nature should never have even existed.

172

CHAPTER 23

Convincing Don

Commander Don Eyb welcomed Tiff into his office and asked how she had been doing.

He had been a serving Police Officer for 42 years and was a long-time member and then Commander of the Mounted Police Unit. As a horseman, his knowledge and expertise were legendary.

It was Don who had choreographed the Sydney Olympic Opening Ceremony performance involving 120 Stockhorses, a world record in its own right. He then worked with all of the horses and riders, training them over many months for their history-making performance.

Tiff had nothing but respect for Don professionally and to top it off he was also a true gentleman. She was honoured to serve in his unit and the thought of leaving this job was almost too much to bear. But the moment she saw Don she had the strangest feeling that everything was going to be okay.

Don was glad to see her back at the stables, but he could tell that she obviously had something on her mind, so he gave her the floor.

Tiff started nervously, explaining that she had doubts about returning and doubts about some of the horses— particularly the young Thoroughbreds. Don started to reply to reassure her that he understood but she continued, so he sat back and listened. She outlined carefully constructed arguments about horse and rider safety as well as the safety of the general public. Then she mentioned Clydesdale-crosses as possible police horses. Don wasn't sure where Tiff was going with this as they had already had three of them in the stables over the years. Sure, it wasn't a particularly high ratio, but it wasn't like they were forbidden. But Tiff was talking about a particular horse, one that she had bought and trained, one that displayed exceptional qualities, and she was asking permission to bring this horse into the troop. Well, that wasn't out of the question, and he couldn't blame her for wanting to ride a horse that she could trust, not after what she'd been through.

Don listened with interest about this amazing horse and how he had recently saved a German tourist. It certainly sounded like he could be very suitable, and he nodded encouragingly. Finally, there was a break in the discussion, so he asked a few questions about his age, height and breeding. He noticed that Tiff was a little evasive in her answers but he didn't push it, thinking that she was just preoccupied.

Finally, he asked her, 'So do you have a photo I can look at?'

Tiff took a deep breath and reached into her pocket, withdrew a photo, and handed it to Don. She looked at the ground, at the door, out the window—anywhere but at Don—and waited for his response.

After a few moments of silence, he spoke up. 'God, he's a bit rough, Tiff.'

It was true and there wasn't much she could say in Toby's defence, but Tiff realised that he could have said a lot worse, so there was hope.

She looked at him imploringly and said, 'Don, his temperament is second to none. He is honestly the best, most willing horse I've ever trained in my life.'

Don thought for a moment. It seemed ludicrous that he should pass up a completely trustworthy horse in favour of a potentially dangerous one based on looks alone.

So, despite the fact that every single cell in his body said 'No', he looked at Tiff and said quietly, 'I suppose we could give him a go.'

Tiff was elated. She drove home on a high and couldn't wait to tell Col. He had thought she was crazy, but she'd proved him wrong.

Sure enough, Col was stunned. He really had to give her credit for her persistence and determination. Nobody else could have done it, but like he said, 'Toby in a photo is a bit different to Toby in real life.'

Tiff didn't tell him that Don had looked a bit shocked when he saw the photo. Maybe she had imagined it but then she remembered his comment about Toby 'being a bit rough' and she embraced reality. It was going to be a long shot but she pushed all doubts out of her mind. She had other things to worry about.

After dinner, she busied herself with filling in Toby's application forms. Everything looked good on paper, except for his questionable breeding, but she had Don's blessing. All she needed to do now was go and get him.

Tiff and Col set off early one Saturday morning, rejoicing in the fact that they had a whole week to spend on the farm relaxing before they brought Toby back. It had been many months since they'd made the trip, and both looked forward to the change of scenery.

When they arrived mid-afternoon, two inquisitive faces greeted them at the front gate. Toby looked gorgeous, a picture of health. Even Jock looked great and definitely not that old. Even though it was winter, the days were glorious—sunny and warm—and the nights cool and cosy. There was still feed in the paddocks.

Tiff told Sid about her plans for Toby. He listened, then started to smile.

'I always knew that horse was going to achieve great things,' he said.

Then his brow slightly creased, and he looked off into the distance. 'But I'm going to miss him,' he said quietly. 'So will Jock; they've become great mates.'

Tiff knew that Sid had become attached to him, and she could understand why. He had recognised Toby's magic long before her and spent many months with him, reinforcing the training she had done. It was going to be a big shock to have him suddenly wrenched away. She started trying to explain why this was happening but he interrupted her.

'Don't worry. I am happy for him. Shit, Tiff, I'm more than happy, it's the best thing in the world. What an opportunity.'

Tiff replied, 'Well, if he doesn't make it, he can come back here until we find him a permanent home.'

But Sid shook his head and said, 'He'll make it—he was born to do this.'

Toby must have been a bit surprised when his rides to the pub suddenly came to an end. He would have become accustomed to his casual, relaxed and predictable lifestyle. There was no hurry, no fuss. In many ways, his life had started to mirror Sid's.

But when Tiff arrived, everything was different. She also seemed different. She was tense and preoccupied. She hurried and spoke little and smiled less. She knew that she was expecting a lot from him and that it was hard for him to adjust to a new set of expectations but she had limited time.

Jock and Sid continued their customary trips to the pub and Tiff was sure Toby wished he could join them. But she was too busy trying to refine his style to let him go off on country jaunts. She taught him to bring his head down and learn what is called 'collection'. She also taught him to leg yield or move off against her leg pressure and to rein back or walk backwards. He was definitely rusty but he was responsive and by the end of the week, she was happy with his progress. She still worried though. Would it be enough?

Tiff realised how much she had invested in this venture, not least her professional integrity. She could very easily emerge from all of this looking like a complete fool, but, if everything worked out, she would have a horse to ride that she trusted implicitly. Most of all she could stay in the Force, and she wouldn't need to sell Toby.

Of course, Toby had no way of understanding any of this. Today was just another day and tomorrow would be a new day, pretty much like today. But he was wrong.

It started raining during the night and within hours the grey skies and gentle rain had became a torrential deluge. The sky was black, and it was cold and miserable. The wind whipped through the trees, stripping them of their remaining leaves and biting the faces of those brave or stupid enough to challenge it.

Toby and Jock stayed in their stable waiting for a break before they would go out to feed. Tiff awoke and cursed her luck. If she had left yesterday, everything would have been fine. They needed to leave today; Col had to be back at work the next day. She listened to the weather report and learned that the bad weather was set to continue for the rest of the week. It rained almost constantly while they packed up their belongings and loaded the car. They ran back and forth balancing their bags and boxes in one hand and a golf umbrella in the other. It rained while they hooked up the float. The mud began to stick to their boots, making the task even harder. Finally, they retreated inside to have a cup of coffee and wait for a break. About two hours later, the rain began to ease to a drizzle and then it stopped. Col and Tiff sprang up, eager to seize the opportunity before it started raining again.

Tiff clipped a lead to Toby's headcollar and led him out of the stable. He looked like he was wondering where on earth she was taking him in this weather. They walked out of the gate and around to the float. She started to lead him up the ramp but he wasn't very keen. She seemed agitated and rushed and he resisted. She persevered and he took a few steps forward, then changed his mind and sidestepped almost onto Col. They tried it again but Toby danced around, not wanting to go anywhere near the float. Tiff asked Col to go and get her a bucket of feed, which he did. She held it in front of Toby, who took a mouthful. Unlike the last time he was floated, Toby wasn't particularly hungry, so this wasn't much of a bribe. The minutes stretched into an hour and they were no closer to getting him loaded. Then the skies began to blacken and a few drops began to fall. Tiffany was almost beside herself. She had wanted to leave that morning and now it was late afternoon. Frantically she tried again and again but it was hopeless; Toby had passed the point of no return. She led him into the paddock and unclipped the rope.

She sat on Sid's porch and put her head in her hands. This was not part of the plan. How would she explain this to Don and how could she expect him to give Toby a chance if she couldn't even get him there?

CHAPTER 24

Pilates

Sid was understanding but philosophical.

'It just wasn't meant to be today. It's been a long time since he was on a float; maybe he just needs a little training.'

He asked Tiff if she wanted him to do a bit of work with Toby, getting him used to the float. Then he remembered the woman in town who specialised in float training.

'You know we could always get Sue out here; she does that fancy stuff with them, you know—Pilates.'

Tiff almost choked on her tea, then took a moment to get the image of Toby doing Pilates out of her head before she could answer him.

'Oh, *Parelli* . . . that's not a bad idea.'

Tiff had met Sue a couple of times and she was an interesting lady. Maybe it would work and even if it didn't, it wouldn't hurt Toby to have another person working with him.

And so, as much as Tiff didn't want to, she admitted defeat and got ready to climb into the car for the trip home. She and Col had a long journey ahead of them and would be very late getting home, so they headed off immediately.

Tiff couldn't believe that after all of this she was going home without Toby and was worried that the whole experience may have damaged his confidence. She realised that she probably should have practised getting him in the float a few days before they had to leave, but it's always easier in hindsight to say what should have been done. She wasn't quite sure what she'd tell Don. She knew it wouldn't sound good if she confessed that she'd been unable to load him.

A few days later, Sue arrived at Jinki with her horse float in tow. She met Toby and liked him immediately. He was friendly and intelligent, and she knew that she wouldn't have much trouble teaching him to load.

Parelli is a program of natural horsemanship, founded in 1981 by American Pat Parelli. The core principle of the Parelli Natural Horsemanship philosophy is that 'Horsemanship can be obtained naturally through communication, understanding, and psychology, versus mechanics, fear and intimidation'.

The movement has many devotees as well as a few critics. Over time it has also devised a float-training system for horses who have problems loading.

The basic premise of the system is to make their life more uncomfortable outside the float than it is inside. This means lunging them in a circle across the ramp of the float, and not allowing them to rest their feet anywhere except on the ramp. As time goes on, the horse is moved further and further up the float and then finally into it.

Toby took very little time to pick up the main message. Soon he began to equate the float with a place of safety rather than danger. After a couple of sessions, he was happily loading and unloading. Sue then took him for a number of short drives to acquaint him with the float's movement and he handled it like a professional.

Meanwhile, back in Sydney, Tiff had decided that honesty was the best policy and explained to Don what had happened when they tried to load Toby. She described the rain and her frame of mind, and added that he was receiving training in the Parelli floating system. She also tried to shoulder some of the blame, saying that she should have done training with him over the week and not left it until the morning they were due to leave.

Don wasn't too perturbed. He knew how difficult horses could be with floats; even some of the older ones played up occasionally. He even told Tiff that, when Toby was ready, she could take a double shift and the police horse float to go to pick him up. Tiff sincerely hoped that he wouldn't regret this kind-hearted gesture when he saw Toby.

Within a week, Tiff received a phone call from Sue telling her that Toby was ready. She set off again, this time feeling confident but at the same time a little apprehensive. The moment of truth was almost upon her: how would people react?

'Well, I'll find out soon enough,' she thought fatalistically. She had done everything she possibly could and now it was up to the universe and Toby to decide . . . although she had no doubts that he would behave impeccably.

Tiff climbed out of the cab, bending and stretching, trying to bring back some feeling into her legs. Ann heard her pull up and came out to meet her, but not before Sid got to her first.

He told Tiff that Toby was fine and that he had done his best to keep up the fancy training she had done with Toby before she left.

Tiff smiled and tried to imagine Toby and Sid riding along in a collected trot on their way to the pub, but she thanked Sid gratefully. She and Toby would need every bit of help they could get to achieve this crazy goal. She went inside to have some lunch and catch up on the local news and fill her mum in on what had been happening at work. She didn't want to get too settled as she had to be back that night. So after some tasty lasagne and crusty garlic bread she gathered up her stuff and headed back to the car.

Tiff opened up the float and held her breath as she led Toby towards the ramp.

He stepped aboard without even a sideways glance and stood waiting for her to tie him up. Once Tiff had gotten over her surprise, she patted him and tied the lead rope loosely to the hook. Even though she was in a hurry, she couldn't help but pause to remember the horse that she had brought to the property just over two years ago. It seemed such a long time ago but also, in some ways, it seemed like yesterday.

Who would have believed that pathetic, half-dead creature would one day be on his way to Sydney to try out as a Mounted Police horse—one of the most demanding and prestigious roles a horse can have? Tiff realised that the odds were still firmly stacked against them, but it was incredible they had gotten this far. She shut the side door firmly and then jumped into the car, trying hard to hold onto hope.

The long drive gave her hours to mull over what could happen. Tiff was able to imagine and rehearse every possible outcome in her mind and it was late evening when they finally arrived at the police stables. By this time her imagination was in overdrive.

Tiff climbed wearily out of the driver's seat and walked around. Just as she had feared, a group of people spilled out of the stable block, eager to meet her and look at the mysterious new recruit. She took a deep breath, backed him out of the float and then waited for their reaction.

Some people said nothing, probably too shocked to speak.

A couple of people sniggered and someone else let out a whistle. Tiff knew this was only a small section of the unit and she'd probably hear much worse tomorrow.

Sadly, Don had gone home for the day. Tiff wished that he'd been able to see Toby before he had a chance to be influenced by other people's opinions. But it wasn't meant to be. When she thought about it, she knew that he would remain impartial and make up his own mind.

So Tiff blocked out the reactions of the others. She was focused on one goal, and nothing was going to distract her from that. She patted Toby to reassure him and started to lead him to his stable for the night.

Toby was wide-eyed; he'd never seen so many people or lights before in his life. But even though he was young and apprehensive, he didn't resist. He trusted Tiff so he followed her obediently. She led him into a building and down a walkway. The floor was hard and unforgiving, and his hooves made a clip-clop sound as he walked along. Other horses poked their heads over their doors as he approached, and he must have felt slightly threatened and quickened his step as a result. He followed Tiffany into a loose box and she closed the door behind them. It smelt strange and it was bright and there were noises he'd never heard before, but he was tired, and the floor inside was soft and spongy. He rested one hind leg as she took off his floating boots and hoisted a rug over his back, fastening it into position. She disappeared for a moment, and he took a drink from a trough in the corner and studied his surroundings. It was a long time since he had been shut in a loose box like this, in the very early days when Tiff was worried about him gorging himself. When she returned, she brought with her a bucket of tasty feed that he ate slowly, and he was left to ponder what had happened to his world.

CHAPTER 25

A bad start

Tiff arrived at work early the next morning, eager to be there when Don met Toby—but she was too late. He had already been in to see him, and he looked grave.

'Well, he's really no better looking in the flesh, is he? In fact, I think he's worse.'

Tiff didn't say anything. She just waited to see what would come next. Don was also waiting for Tiff to say something, so there was an uncomfortable silence for a few moments.

Eventually, Don spoke up, 'I don't know, Tiff. I just don't know.'

Well, that's better than a flat-out refusal, thought Tiff. *Now for the next step.* 'Why don't I show you what he can do?' she asked Don.

Don nodded as though he was expecting her to say that. They walked down to Toby's box in silence and Tiff went in to get him. She brought him outside and a new crowd of people gathered around to check him out.

There were a couple of surprised gasps but in general people were silent, maybe because Don was there. The only person to speak up was Julia, a veteran of ten years. She told Tiff that Toby was possibly one of the ugliest horses she'd ever seen and that they would be a laughing-stock with him in their ranks.

Tiff didn't say anything but continued saddling up.

Julia's words hurt. Tiff didn't think Toby would lower the standard of the troop. The public loved all the police horses, and they would love Toby too. In her eyes, he was a magnificent, kind, beautiful horse and, she felt, in time the others would feel the same.

Finally, Tiff turned around and snapped at Julia, 'Why don't you ride him, and then you'll see why I think he'll be perfect?'

Julia grumbled something in reply and then agreed. She led Toby out of the stables and into the exercise yard. She gathered up the reins and put one foot into the stirrup, then hoisted herself into the saddle. She pushed her heels into his sides to tell him to move on.

Toby stood there for a moment. Julia was far heavier than anyone he'd ever carried before, and he wasn't happy.

Sid and Tiff were about 65 and 70 kilograms each but Julia was around 90 kilograms. She put Toby into a walk and then into a trot and then the unthinkable happened. Toby began to buck; he gave two sharp, violent bucks before he completely unseated Julia and threw her to the ground. He galloped off to the other side of the yard and stood there, head down with a guilty look on his face.

Tiff stood there, unable to believe what was happening. She had closed her eyes then opened them again at the last minute, just in time to see Julia hit the ground and roll over. Surely she was dreaming; it had to be a nightmare, a horrible slow-motion nightmare. She looked around at the other people and saw the stunned looks on their faces. This was no dream. Julia was lying there moaning, her arm twisted into a strange position, looking completely useless. A couple of people ran over to her but Tiff just stood there, unable to move, think or speak. Eventually, she went and got Toby and led him back to the stable. She didn't talk to him. She was so confused that there was nothing she could say. All she knew was that this was far worse than the worst possible scenario she had imagined on the drive down. She had not predicted anything even half as bad as this.

Toby had never bucked, never put a foot wrong in his life, and now, the one time she needed him to be on his best behaviour, he did this. And in front of Don, who had been so generous. Sure, the last few days had been unsettling, but he was not the sort of horse to be ruffled by things like that, especially not to this extent. She considered the weight factor and decided that it must have been the problem. Toby was unaccustomed to carrying that extra weight and he had fought against it.

Tiff cursed herself for not thinking of it before she had opened her big mouth. When she thought back over what had happened, she really couldn't believe she had done what she did. For her to suggest Julia ride him was a crazy idea. If only she could turn back time. If only there was an undo button.

In the back of Tiff's mind, another explanation was also forming, one that was too ridiculous to consider seriously but it stayed there, playing with her conscience. Julia had been openly hostile in her feelings about Toby and had got into the saddle with an extremely negative attitude. What if Toby had picked up on this? Even crazier was the thought that maybe Toby had actually understood what Julia had said about him and decided to pay her back.

Tiff looked at him and gave him a pat.

'Who knows what goes on in your mind,' she said and began to unsaddle him.

There was no point trying to understand any of this; they had blown their chance in a spectacular fashion and now Tiff needed to repair the damage done to her professional reputation.

It was so hard to accept that it was all over. She had been on such a high these past few weeks believing that soon she would be able to see Toby every day. That she could ride him, and he could help restore her faith and her confidence.

When Tiff had settled Toby, she walked back to the group. She wasn't looking forward to facing everyone again. Someone had taken Julia to hospital and the conversation was still very much focused on dissecting the incident. Everyone had an opinion but, strangely enough, nobody was openly hostile about Toby as Tiff had expected. She didn't offer any defence as she thought it would make her sound guilty or desperate, neither of which was particularly appealing to her. Eventually the conversation returned to more mundane topics and the incident was politely 'forgotten'.

Tiff went out on patrol and when she came back to the barracks later that afternoon, Don had already left for the day. She was disappointed as she really wanted to talk to him, even though she didn't know what she would say. Instead, she went home and told Col all about it. He was stunned. It was the last thing he would have expected of Toby also.

'I thought his looks would have been his undoing, not his behaviour,' he said in disbelief. 'Well, you tried, and I think you did well to get this far.'

Tiff nodded, although it didn't make her feel any better. This was not how it was meant to be. Toby was not danger-ous or badly schooled. He was an incredible horse and now nobody would ever know. She climbed wearily into bed but slept fitfully.

It was the first thing Tiff thought of when she opened her eyes, and she was forced to accept that it had indeed happened. It wasn't some horrible dream that she could forget and now she had to face the music. She also needed to decide whether she would stay a Mountie now that she couldn't use Toby. The previous day had been incredibly difficult. She had expected to ride Toby but then had had to ride another horse instead. Her stress left her barely able to think straight and nearly physically sick. She didn't know how she would have reacted if the horse had been difficult or there had been a dangerous situation. Luckily it had been an uneventful day.

Tiff expected to see Don the next morning when she arrived at work, but he was absent, and she was unsure of what to do next. Should she make arrangements to get Toby transported back to her property at Maraylya or would it be okay to leave him here another day?

Tiff was crushed that she had invested so much time and effort and it had all come to nothing. She couldn't believe that, after everything, she hadn't even got a chance to ride Toby herself.

Then suddenly she got an urge to do exactly that . . .

CHAPTER 26

(Unofficial) first day

Tiff considered the situation.

Toby had not received any official rejection. In fact, the last conversation she had had with Don was to confirm that he was on a trial. There was no reason that Tiff could see why she could not ride him today, so she saddled him up and headed over to the office to check the roster. She had been paired with Sue and Echo, who was a quiet, experienced horse, perfect for this assignment. She told the grooms of her change of plans and then informed Sue, who stared at her in disbelief. But she knew it was pointless to argue with Tiff and before long the four of them headed out for a day on the beat.

Toby handled the day with the confidence and self-assurance of a veteran and Tiff was delighted, although not surprised. He wasn't rattled by the traffic or noise and seemed to enjoy the attention he received from the public. It was interesting that for the first time in his life people did not see him as ugly. To these 'lay' people he was a beautiful, majestic police horse. People seemed to trust the police horses and even people who were typically afraid of horses would step forwards confidently for a pat.

Toby looked stunning in his police gear and stood proudly as people patted his neck and face. He plodded around for the rest of the day unfazed by anything, enjoying the sights, the company and the adoration. Luckily there were no riots, assaults, robberies or other serious police work. They just walked around the streets of Redfern, chatting and interacting with the public.

As the afternoon wore on, Tiff breathed a sigh of relief that she hadn't received any call back to base for a dressing-down. It was no secret that she had taken Toby out and surely if there was a problem she would have been recalled. She headed back to the stables feeling a little more buoyant than when she had left. It did help that Sue was impressed with Toby and had remarked that he hadn't put a foot wrong all day. Tiff was glad of her support. It might prove to be a valuable asset if needed later.

Don was still not at the stables. He had not been in all day, so Tiff was once again unsure of what to do next. But she didn't get much time to think about that as the moment her colleagues saw her, they grilled her on how they had fared. She suspected a few of them didn't believe her when she sang Toby's praises. So they turned to Sue, who also launched into a gushing account of Toby's virtues. A few people seemed to realise that they were both telling the truth and congratulated Tiff on not only starting and training Toby, but also having the courage to bring him in. They had been there the day that she had been thrown at the Easter Show and genuinely wanted her to stay, even if that meant riding a horse who was odd-looking, to say the least. They also realised that they would not have to ride him, so it was no reflection on them.

Tiff finally began to feel a glimmer of hope. It was so badly needed after the last twenty-four hours. She decided that she would ride Toby again tomorrow, even if Don was there. She just wouldn't mention it and hoped he would do the same. She checked the roster to see who she was on with and it was Bodie. Perfect: another sensible horse. She thanked the others for their support and led Toby off down the corridor to his box and began to unsaddle him.

It was the end of Toby's first (unofficial) day as a troop horse. She couldn't believe it. She stood there looking at him and he turned to stare back at her. For a moment their eyes locked, and she remembered the dream she had the night after she first saw him.

In it, he had stood proudly, surrounded by a mass of admiring strangers. At the time the dream seemed totally ridiculous but today it had become a reality. Tiff was a little unnerved as she had never had prophetic dreams before. She couldn't get it out of her mind, and she thought back to that day. She had always thought that she had gone to the farm to buy Bundy. Toby was just an afterthought. She now wondered whether the real reason she picked up the newspaper that morning, why she scanned the ads so intently, was that she was meant to save Toby.

Even harder to believe was the fact that only three years later, he would return the favour and save her from herself and the demons that were destroying her confidence and spirit.

The next day when Tiff saw Don she wasn't sure what to expect. She had various explanations at the ready and decided to just see what his reaction was before picking the best response. But he said nothing. He greeted her but didn't mention Toby.

What the hell does that mean? Tiff thought. Should she broach the subject with Don or leave it alone? Continue riding Toby or leave him for the day and not push her luck? She had never been so confused in her life. Surely if Don wanted Toby out of the stables, he would have demanded it by now?

Don never did ask for Toby to be removed, and the incident that first day was not mentioned again.

Tiff decided that Toby was officially now on trial but she was acutely aware that, should he make even the slightest mistake, he would be out. Don had already given him one second chance and would not do so again. She was beyond grateful for that chance.

As she walked to get him, the other horses poked their heads over their doors to greet her. Gorgeous horses who had been purposely bred and were worth large sums of money.

Tiff arrived at Toby's box and looked in at him, her rescue horse. Finishing off the last scraps of his breakfast, part of his forelock obscuring his eyes, totally oblivious to the crazy set of circumstances that had carried him along to this point in life. She smiled. As long as she lived, Tiff suspected that she would never totally understand the enigma that was Toby.

CHAPTER 27

The trial

So began the most stressful three months of Tiff's life. She had learned from the experience with Julia that she needed to be constantly on guard, to really think about every situation and not leave anything to chance.

Toby began his trial with regular patrols as well as training in the many disciplines he needed to become a fully-fledged police horse. As a rough guide, for every ten horses that are trialled, only one is chosen. It is a rare combination of skills, attributes and temperament that makes a good police horse.

Toby had no idea of what this new life held for him. All he knew was that there were more horses here than he had ever seen in his life and that he was treated well. He received five meals a day, he was stabled and rugged, groomed, exercised, clipped and wormed, and also shod every five weeks. And then of course there was the attention he received. For a young, smart horse it was the perfect lifestyle, all the more incredible considering where Toby had come from.

As a police horse, Toby would always work with another horse. This is an occupational health and safety requirement for the riders and the horses, as well as the general public. As a new recruit he would start doing quiet patrol work around the back streets of Redfern and then, as his confidence increased, be introduced to busier streets with more traffic. He would work on the left-hand side of a more experienced horse to shield him until he was more confident. As time went on, he would be taken into the city during the day and again into the city at night. Finally, he would gradually be exposed to a demonstration or crowd-control situation.

Police horses are highly valued in crowd control and routine patrols because it is estimated that one horse and rider are equivalent to ten officers on foot. That means if you have ten horses, you have the equivalent of a hundred officers. Mounted Police have a distinct height advantage and can easily spot the cause of a disturbance in a crowd; if required, they can take immediate action to extricate an offender. The horses are specially trained in pairs to walk either side of a suspect, allowing the officers to guide them to a police truck or car. Sometimes just the presence of an officer on a horse has a calming effect on large groups of people.

Toby would work four days a week, Thursday to Sunday, and be exercised for 40 minutes a day, with trot and canter work, on the other three days. In peak condition, he would be spelled for approximately six weeks a year at a farm at Colo in the Hawkesbury Valley. He would also learn the manoeuvres and drill movements needed for him to perform such things as the musical ride. Even after his initial training, Toby would receive ongoing education to refresh his memory. At least three days a month (usually Wednesdays) were dedicated to training.

Toby responded impeccably to every situation he encountered in the three months of his trial. His easygoing nature impressed most of the other officers and grooms and they all felt he was a real asset to the troop. But there were a few people who maintained that he really wasn't police horse material. They didn't deny that his disposition was perfect for the role; they just didn't think he looked the part.

One day Tiff was on patrol with one of these officers, Griffo. They were having a friendly debate about it when Tiff suggested they go into nearby Centennial Park and ask people what they thought. Griffo was supremely confident that a large number of people would agree with him.

Centennial Parklands is an equestrian centre within the grounds of Centennial Park. People can agist their horses there and use the facilities or hire horses and have lessons. On this particular beautiful spring day, people were out enjoying the sunshine, and it was a hive of activity. The horses were all primped and preened, and the riders matched their mounts in their immaculate white jodhpurs and button-up shirts.

Tiff and Toby and Griffo and Ras rode up to a small group, then made some light conversation.

Finally Tiff asked them, 'I'm really interested in your opinion. What do you think of this horse? Do you think he is good-looking?'

People seemed a little taken aback. A few shifted uncomfortably in their saddles, then someone spoke up. 'I think he's cute.'

Tiff was a little surprised but at least she hadn't said he was ugly. All of the other riders started nodding in agreement, pleased that someone had found the right words. They moved onto another group and again there seemed to be a unanimous verdict that Toby was 'cute'. As they were leaving the park, they rode over to a third group of people and unbelievably they all stated the same thing. Tiff burst out laughing at this point and began to suspect that 'cute' wasn't quite as pleasant as it sounded—it was probably a euphemism for something far less desirable.

Sure enough, when they got back to the stables that afternoon, they looked up the meaning of 'cute' and discovered the Australian urban meaning of cute was 'ugly but interesting'. Griffo was ecstatic—every single person had in effect said he was ugly—but Tiff wouldn't concede. In good humour, she informed him that they hadn't used the word 'ugly', so it didn't count. Deep down, however, she knew it was true. He wasn't going to win any beauty contest, but it didn't matter to her. She was sure the majority of people, non-horse people, would think he was beautiful and that was the only thing that mattered.

Toby seemed to enjoy his job, which made him a pleasure to work with. He was enthusiastic and keen, and a fast learner. He also possessed the ability to figure things out and would persevere with something long after other horses gave up.

All of the horse boxes had a single bolt on them. Some horses learn that, if they fiddle with this bolt with their lips, they can open it. These horses then have a second bolt added to the door about halfway down and this usually stops them. But horses like Toby, who manage to undo this second bolt, need a third bolt added, down almost at ground level. Until Toby arrived on the scene, no horse had ever managed to undo all three bolts. Toby persisted and learned that if he stood on the kickboard, just inside the door, and stretched his neck as far as he could, he could reach the third bolt. And with some stretching and manoeuvring of his lips, he could undo it. This feat earned him the nickname of

'MacGyver' after the TV character who has a penchant for escaping sticky situations.

When the other horses escaped, they usually started cleaning up the spilt feed and hay that was left lying around the stable block, but not Toby. Sure, he might grab a few mouthfuls of feed on his way, but his destination was clear. He would set off at a brisk pace, out of the stable block, around the corner and up to the sand yard for a roll. Tiff decided that it must have had to do with his trips to the beach in his early days. She thought it funny that they were both beach bums, with her also spending her youth on the coast—on the northern beaches of Sydney.

There was no official swearing-in of Toby. Not even a formal recognition that he had made the grade. He simply became a member of the troop. Troop horse Toby was his name, and he gained a shiny nameplate that hung on his stable door. This was the only official acknowledgement of his acceptance into the oldest continuous mounted unit in the world. But that in no way undermined the achievement.

It was an honour bestowed on very few.

CHAPTER 28

Twelve months

By mid-2004, Toby had been introduced to most of the major ceremonies that he would participate in, including the Gay and Lesbian Mardi Gras, the City to Surf fun run and New Year's Eve celebrations. All of them came and went without even the slightest reaction from him. He was brave and sensible, the perfect combination for a police horse, plus he genuinely liked people and seemed to enjoy interacting with the public.

Tiff had grown along with Toby, in confidence and perception. She had learned so much about her role, the people she served and the horses. As she regained her confidence, she began to take on more responsibilities. Even Toby was assigned more challenging duties.

It had been a remarkable twelve months.

Tiff wondered where she would have been if it hadn't worked out. How she would have coped riding horses she didn't know, when she was in such a frail state.

She bent down to pat his neck, to convey some of the gratitude she felt for him, when she noticed that he was making a strange movement. They were riding through Kings Cross, approaching an intersection and a Gloria Jean's coffee shop. The shop was playing music out onto the footpath.

Tiff wondered whether Toby had picked up a stone in his hoof or something but then she noticed the strangest thing: after a few strides, she realised that his peculiar swagger seemed to be in time to the music. At first she doubted it but the closer they came to the speaker, the more pronounced it became. As they moved away, out of range of the music, the swagger ceased. She started to think that she was going a little crazy when it came to Toby and that she needed to get a grip on reality, so she dismissed it. Horses could not possess an appreciation of music.

But sure enough the following week, he repeated his performance and the police officer who was with them even remarked on it. Eventually it became common practice for him to do his 'jive' every time they passed the shop.

It was no wonder that Tiff woke most mornings keen to get to work and couldn't wait to get in the saddle.

How could she be sad or fearful when she spent her days with the most wonderful, funny companion? Sometimes she did think back to the accident, but it didn't fill her with dread like it used to. And she didn't relive those terrifying thoughts of impending death over and over anymore.

Toby had certainly been her saviour. Gentle, kind Toby who carried Tiff everywhere and whom she trusted implicitly. Sometimes she almost had to pinch herself to believe it was real. This life, this amazing life, with the most amazing horse.

What had she done to deserve it? To deserve him?

CHAPTER 29

The Military Tattoo

Two blue lines. Tiff looked at them for a few seconds then checked the box. She looked at them again and brought the box closer to compare. Yep, there were still two lines. She waited to see if one would disappear, but it didn't. She read the instructions again and then rechecked the lines. It was at this point that she began to suspect that she might be pregnant.

There was another test in the box so she decided that these things mustn't be very accurate and that's why there were two. She took the second test.

Two lines appeared immediately.

Tiff did the calculations and came to an ominous conclusion.

Shit!

She had been in disbelief when she first learned that the Edinburgh Military Tattoo was coming to Australia, and Mounted Police were going to participate. It would be only the second time the Tattoo was performed outside Scotland; as a rider, it would be the pinnacle of Tiff's career. Performing under lights, in front of thousands—millions— of people, because it was going to be televised around the world. Tiff couldn't believe that only ten years ago she had been a horse-crazy kid riding Tia around the Northern Beaches of Sydney. Now this . . . and with Toby.

Toby had been selected to perform along with fifteen other horses. Technically he was still an apprentice, but everyone was impressed with his calm disposition and thought he would be a wonderful addition to the team. Surprisingly, nobody objected on the grounds of his appearance. If ever he was going to embarrass the unit with his big, plain head, it would be at a performance in front of a worldwide audience.

The Military Tattoo has a long history. It was inspired by a show that was performed at the Ross Bandstand, below Edinburgh Castle, in 1949. Since that time, it has grown into an annual event watched by a worldwide television audience of approximately 10 million. The backdrop for the spectacular event is the 1000-year-old castle, which looms imposingly over the performances.

In 2005, when the event came to Sydney, a full-sized replica of the castle's gatehouse and ramparts was created in a former railway workshop in Newtown. It was the largest outdoor theatrical set ever constructed in Australia. All of the original features were re-created, with mock cannons, flaming beacons and an extravagant light show. The performers included drummers, military units, fiddlers, dancers, bagpipes and of course the New South Wales Mounted Police performing their musical ride.

They had been practising for months, three times a week, learning the complex manoeuvres by heart, perfecting the timing so that the cross-overs were faultless. Not only did the riders know the routine, but so did the horses.

Tiff had once been a part of a ride at the Sydney Easter Show where one of the riders had fallen off. The rider had scrambled out the way and her horse continued on in the line-up, keeping up with the others and performing all of the steps riderless. That's not to say that the horses don't need their riders. His speed was off so he began to fall behind and he didn't stay in perfectly straight lines, but it was a clear indicator of the intelligence of the police horses. The rider managed to grab him on his next pass, and she scrambled aboard, and they finished the ride together.

Tiff looked at the pregnancy test in her hand.

It was September. The Tattoo was in February 2005 and Tiff had just calculated that her baby was due in May. She would be too pregnant, way too pregnant, to ride. She couldn't believe it. This was all she had thought about for months, and now it was never going to happen.

Tiff was conflicted. She loved children. She loved her work as a nanny and had always dreamed of having her own children. Just not now! She felt incredibly guilty that she had received one of the ultimate blessings in life and she was unhappy at the timing. So many people never got the opportunity to become parents and here she was, distressed.

She weighed up the situation and decided that nothing, not even the Military Tattoo, was going to stop her enjoying this pregnancy, this baby.

Nothing . . . except maybe gestational diabetes.

It started at about 20 weeks, when Tiff noticed an excessive thirst and started to put on weight at an alarming rate. Before long her colleagues began to notice and even started joking that she had 'cankles', saying her knees had reached her ankles. Luckily Tiff could take a joke, so she never took offence, but she did feel somewhat justified when she was diagnosed at 26 weeks. But it was no cause for celebration.

A diet change didn't work and Tiff became insulin dependent. The rest of her pregnancy revolved around finger pricking and insulin injections, which she had to give to herself in her thigh. The romanticised view of pregnancy that she had always held simply didn't align with her reality. She was big, uncomfortable and feeling useless.

In the early stages of her pregnancy (up until twelve weeks), Tiff was allowed to ride on patrol work but after that she could only ride within the compound, in fatigues, not in her full uniform and without her gun. She could exercise horses until she decided to stop or until her doctor ordered otherwise. She rode Toby for some of the practices for the Military Tattoo but eventually had to step aside.

At that point she became a support person for the unit, performing admin duties, answering phones, doing tour groups and cleaning gear.

It was incredibly hard, standing on the sidelines on opening night, watching all of the horses and riders file into the arena. She was with them in spirit, feeling what they were feeling but, at the same time, strangely disconnected. She felt a kick and remembered the reason she was not out there with them, and an odd thought popped into her mind: her baby had ridden before it was even born. She felt a pang of jealousy. She wished she could have ridden before she was born too.

Then, just as she was standing there, lost in thought, it happened.

Toby had started out okay but, as the minutes ticked on, he became rattled. While he was used to other riders, this was an incredibly demanding situation. It was one thing to practise the drill but another to be performing it in front of thousands of people and under lights. When the riders began cantering through the cross-over, the unthinkable happened. He stopped. He refused to go through. All of the other horses and riders backed up behind him and there was chaos.

Tiff stood there horrified. *No, no, no.* What was he doing? She was terrified that he would lose it or that some of the other horses would lose it, turning what was already a bad situation into a full-blown catastrophe. She held her breath and willed him to settle, hoping that it was just a one-off.

The troop regrouped and continued; luckily, the remainder of the presentation was perfect. Tiff felt the colour slowly return to her face and her heart begin to beat normally again. She was sure she had aged ten years in the past six minutes.

Toby didn't participate in any of the remaining five performances. While it was disappointing, he was still a relative newcomer to the unit and so it was understandable.

It was a gentle reminder that, while Toby was remarkable, he was not infallible.

CHAPTER 30

Roan

There was a joke that used to make its way around the police stables that the only way a good police horse could leave was if it went lame or changed colour.

Many horses did leave because of lameness but no one had ever tested the other option. That was until Toby.

Good police horses are hard to find. It's little wonder then that, once they are fully trained, they are almost irreplaceable. But the work they perform is physically hard and sometimes issues arise. Any lameness is thoroughly investigated and most times the horse is immediately retired.

When Toby arrived at the stables in 2003, he was a rich bay in colour with a broken white stripe down his face. His roman nose was obvious to those who knew horses and he also had three white socks, not four, which would have been more uniform (and preferable). There was one other thing about him that was unusual. He had freckles inside his nostrils. While they were not glaringly obvious, they were a harbinger of what was to come.

After a couple of years in the Force, people had become accustomed to his looks. He was just Toby, an agreeable, unflappable member of the troop who had a unique outlook on life and some very amusing characteristics. But around 2005 he started to change . . .

It started with a few white hairs on a brush, nothing major, but then there were a few more. Tiff was a little confused but not alarmed. Horses don't miraculously change colour. But as time went by, the spread of white hairs only seemed to intensify. They weren't patches but individual hairs diffused throughout his coat. He was turning roan.

Roan is a coat colour where there is a mixture of white and pigmented hairs. The roan colour is often not obvious until the foal has had its first shed. Toby by this stage was nearly six years old. Tiff couldn't believe it but then, like everything else with this horse, she sort of could. It was as if he hadn't shocked the establishment enough with his arrival a few years earlier, so he decided to shock it some more.

Tiff ignored it and so did everyone else, much like the emperor's new clothes, but eventually it reached a stage where it could no longer be overlooked. Not only had white hairs overtaken his once brown coat but his freckles began to move up from his muzzle and spread all over his face too.

If it hadn't been such a serious issue, it would have been funny, but this was grave. There had never been a roan police horse; it was unheard of. How could Toby stay in the Force now?

Surprisingly, Toby did. His natural aptitude for the job was so great that even the curious feat of changing colour had no effect on his tenure. While his colour was openly discussed and became the butt of more than a few jokes, he stayed on as one of the most highly regarded horses in the troop.

Always one to test the limits, Toby had proved that the old colour-changing rumour was simply not true.

CHAPTER 31

Jock and Clyde

Tiff had just put her key in the ignition when the phone rang. She reached over and fumbled around in her handbag. It was barely dawn and she wondered who on earth would be calling at this time of the morning. She finally found it just as the last ring played. It was her mother, so she called her back, her heart racing as to the reason for the call.

'Ah, Tiffy,' said Ann. 'I wanted to catch you before you left for work. Jock's dead.'

'What?' said Tiff, stunned.

'Well, he'd been unwell for a couple of weeks now. Mary's been out, running tests, checking bloods, you know. I think it was cancer but I don't know where. Anyway, he got weaker and weaker, and yesterday's bloods were really bad. He had virtually no white blood cells left. Sid wouldn't let Mary euthanise him and I just heard the gunshot.'

This was not uncommon. A lot of country people preferred to shoot their animals. It was instant and, if they were companion animals, considered the last good deed that could be done for them. Vets sometimes had trouble finding a vein, especially in very sick animals, and it was distressing for the animal and owner to have to repeatedly jab them.

Tiff's mind was already racing to the next worrying question, 'How's Sid?'

'Not good. He hasn't said much, and I haven't seen him this morning.'

'I'll try to come up on the weekend. I don't know what I can do but I'd like to try.'

Tiff drove to work in disbelief. How could this happen and why did it always happen to animals that were so loved, so cherished? Jock wasn't young but he still should have had years of life left to enjoy. She was also seriously worried about Sid. His health wasn't great, mentally or physically.

Friday afternoon she set off, reaching Jinki late at night.

Ann handed Tiff a coffee and they sat in the kitchen for an hour or so, catching up. She was thrilled by the prospect of becoming a grandmother and wanted to know how the pregnancy was going and how Tiff was coping at work. She'd already heard about Toby's antics at the Military

Tattoo and thought it was funny. 'He didn't want to do it without his mumma,' she said.

'Well, he's going to have to get used to it when I'm on maternity leave,' said Tiff.

Eventually the conversation turned to the real reason Tiff had visited. 'It's only been a few months since we were here at Christmas and Jock was fine then.'

'I think sometimes cancer lies dormant for a while, then for whatever reason it just takes hold,' replied Ann.

Late the next morning Tiff saw Sid sitting on a bench in the sun and she went over to him. He glanced up and nodded then pulled a cigarette from his pack and lit it. They sat there in silence for a while then he said, 'He had a good life . . . I just wish it had been a bit longer.'

'I know, Sid—so do I,' said Tiff.

They talked about what had happened and the pain of losing a horse. Tiff was surprised by how open he was and was glad she had made the trek. She knew that Sid would only feel comfortable talking to someone who understood horses and who had experienced the bond.

'What a shame Toby's in the Force now. You could have had him,' said Tiff, acutely aware of the timing. 'Only a few years ago, he was still here.'

'No, I'm glad he's there. What an honour, hey,' said Sid, his eyes a little misty at the thought of his old mate.

'What about Bundy? I could bring him up,' said Tiff.

'Too much horse for me,' replied Sid. 'I'm not as fit as I used to be. Anyway, I told you, he's a dickhead, and I don't have Jock to keep him in line.'

Tiff laughed and even Sid smiled a little.

'I'll be okay. I can't replace Jock and I don't want to. I've had a good innings. Think it's time to just let things lie.'

Tiff was alarmed but she didn't want to make a big deal out of anything in case he shut her out. She took him down to the pub for lunch and got him a few groceries on the way home and they talked a lot about Toby.

She left the next morning, hoping Sid would be okay and that this wouldn't foreshadow a decline in his health.

She knew all too well that when you love an animal like Sid loved Jock, their loss can be crushing. Jock was a part of his identity and now, with him gone, Sid was struggling to know who he was. Like he said to her, 'I feel like I'm missing an arm or a leg.' Tiff had replied, 'No, it's a part of your heart.'

She knew he was blaming himself for not picking up on the cancer sooner and not being able to stop it. He was angry and sad and fearful of a future that didn't contain Jock. She wondered if he would ever be happy again.

The months went by and while she thought about Sid often, she was so unwell with her pregnancy that it was impossible to drive up to Jinki. Now, in her final trimester, she finally began to feel a bit more human. She was determined to make this trip in case she became housebound when the baby arrived.

The tree-lined driveway was a welcome sight after so many hours on the road. Ann and Errol came out to help her unload and then from around the back of the car appeared Sid.

Ann had kept Tiff updated on his slide into the abyss and then his marathon climb back out. The days and weeks of drinking sun-up to sundown, his only respite being a few hours sleep when he passed out unconscious. His haggard, haunted eyes revealing the depth of his troubled soul, angry and enraged at an invisible foe. And then finally, quiet acceptance and a gradual softening.

Sid was pleased to see her, but Tiff could feel his impatience. She followed him down the laneway until they reached a paddock that contained the most magnificent Clydesdale gelding she had ever seen. Deep bay in colour, eyes totally obscured by a luscious lock of black hair, a splendid cresty neck and fluffy, feathery white fetlocks. His back was broad and inviting. He was simply divine in every aspect.

'I've always wanted one, you know . . . and then one day I just thought, why not?'

'Why not indeed?' said Tiff. 'He's stunning, I'm so jealous.' Then she added, 'Does he even notice you up there? I think you'll need to eat a bit more.'

'I've been training him for a few weeks now. He's smart. Not as smart as your young fellow but pretty good. Actually, he reminds me a bit of Toby. He's got that "old soul" feel about him.'

'Not like the other young dickhead,' Tiff laughed.

She was overjoyed to see how well Sid was doing. Starting and training a young horse was just the elixir he needed. And what a horse he was.

'What's his name?' she asked.

'Clyde.'

'Wow, that's original.'

Tiff spent many lazy hours sitting in the sun, watching Sid work his magic with Clyde. Just like her, he was in a different place when he was training horses. Well, maybe not so much a place but a different dimension.

Happy with his progress for the day, Sid led Clyde over to the fence and tied him loosely, then started to untack him.

Tiff spoke up, finally raising something that had been on her mind for a while.

'Toby and I marched in the Anzac Day Parade last year.'

'Yes, I know. Ann told me. I bet he was amazing.'

'He was. It was!' she said, remembering the emotion. 'Sid, I've never felt anything like what I felt that day. Seeing all those men and women. Why don't you come down and march next year? You can stay with Col and me.'

Sid looked at her. Tiff could tell he was thinking about what to say but there was too much emotion, confusion and heartache for him to put any of it into words. Finally, he just said, 'Nah, not for me. Too many people.'

He could see her disappointment. It obviously meant a lot to her, but it was simply not possible, so he added, 'Next year, when you and Toby march, you march for me.'

CHAPTER 32

Cronulla

Tiff had been home a few weeks but was still in absolute awe. How could something so perfect, so full of life and so noisy not have even existed ten months ago?

They had called her Brianna and when Tiff looked at her, she knew her life was never going to be the same. She felt different—settled and content in a way she had never felt before. Sure, she had been nervous those first few days, but she found that after spending her life caring for animals, caring for a small human was not that much different.

Tiff was also keen to finally settle into their new home on 18 hectares they had recently purchased at Bilpin in the Blue Mountains. With her job and then the later stages of pregnancy, many of the things she had wanted to do had been left undone. Now was a great time to do them. Ben had recently been retired up to Jinki, but she was still competing with Bundy and had Flame (Col's horse for the moment) at home, so it wasn't long before she was back in the saddle. She had thought that she would miss work and the routine, but she didn't. In fact, she was quite happy at home and determined to make the most of her maternity leave.

The only thing Tiff did miss was Toby. She missed everything about him. It did help that another police officer, Kylie, had taken a shine to him and was keen to ride him while Tiff was away.

Tiff was beginning to realise that Toby's worth was far greater than she had ever imagined. She had brought him into the unit to help her regain her confidence but as time went by more and more people wanted to ride him. Generally, it was officers who were just starting in the unit—keen but not completely at ease. She always said yes and was proud that he was helping other people and serving the community. But in some ways, it was like cutting the apron strings with a child. She missed their closeness and the dependency that he once bestowed on her. Yet she rationalised that he seemed to enjoy his work and not only would it be boring for him to come home with her and stand around doing nothing but also a waste of his gifts.

While Toby was renowned in the unit for being soft and gentle, he also possessed a mental toughness that was an invaluable asset in high-stress situations.

Marches and demonstrations—and their violent cousin, the riot—are one of the most dangerous aspects of a police horse's life. Only horses who have the mental strength and stamina to cope are used and then only after much training.

Tiff wasn't sure how Toby would cope but, in his first year, he attended a few marches and seemed unfazed. The yelling, chanting and swell of people as they surged along the route barely seemed to register as anything abnormal to him.

Later he was dispatched to a couple of peaceful demonstrations and again he took them all in his stride. Tiff wasn't the only one who noticed his calm and accepting manner, which was incredible considering his young age. The other officers and even Don, the Commander of the unit, were also impressed. Tiff finally began to feel some validation of her decision to bring Toby into the Force. Until that point, there were still a few people who felt he was an outsider. Now it was almost unanimous that he was not only part of the troop but also extremely valuable.

In the early 2000s, there were numerous demonstrations against the Iraq war, globalisation and the usual May Day marches. Toby began to cover more and more demonstrations. Tiff always felt safe up astride her 'giant packhorse' who listened to directions and worked as part of the team.

But no one had any idea just how valuable he was until 11 December 2005, when he and another horse, Dollar Mick, and two officers were sent to the coastal suburb of Cronulla to monitor some racial unrest that had been building over the previous week.

It was a Sunday morning and the two officers unloaded Toby and Mick from the float. By midday they found themselves in the middle of a full-scale riot—it was as though war had erupted on the streets of Sydney. They had already radioed for backup and the Commander of the Mounted Police Unit and another officer quickly loaded more horses and drove to the scene.

Five thousand people, fuelled by alcohol, a Sydney radio shock-jock's incendiary comments and racial tensions that had been simmering for weeks, began to turn on each other, the police, ambulance officers and anyone who got in their way. The Mounted Police in their riot gear, the Riot Squad and ordinary officers attempted to form a line to push rioters back and protect the people who were being threatened. In turn, they were pelted with bottles and any other ammunition the rioters could get their hands on.

It was one of the most dangerous situations a police horse and officer could find themselves in; for Toby, with just over two years of service under saddle, it was extraordinary that he managed to cope. He was hit by projectiles multiple times but never panicked or lost his nerve.

227

Over the next eight hours, Toby kept calm and focused, and continued to do what was asked of him unquestioningly. All of his training came to the fore, and he worked tirelessly assisting to break up the crowds of people and restore peace. But no amount of training could have prepared a horse for this situation. It was beyond anything anyone had ever experienced.

At one point the Mounted Police horses had to provide a safe convoy for an ambulance. It was attempting to transport injured people from the North Cronulla Surf Life Saving Club to hospital when it was attacked and the paramedics issued a Code One. The police horses and their riders led from the front and also protected the ambulance from the rear on its journey.

On that day, Toby proved his worth to the unit, the community and the country. If ever there was an instance that proved that a handsome appearance and fancy pedigree paled into insignificance in the face of real danger, it was now. No monetary value could be placed on bravery and now no value could ever be placed on Toby. He was simply irreplaceable.

Luckily, none of the horses was injured, but upon returning to the stables that night, it became apparent that Dollar Mick was suffering from extreme stress. The grooms cared for him and he did not return the next day when eight horses and riders including Toby and Tiff (who was called in from maternity leave) were dispatched to Cronulla.

That day saw no repeat of the violence and hostility that had escalated so badly the day before. The police patrolled the streets and beaches, speaking to people and trying to gauge the mood of the area, always at the ready.

Tiff was glad to be back in the saddle even if it was not the gentle start back to her job that she had been expecting.

Sadly, Dollar Mick never really got over his involvement in the Cronulla riots. He still worked as a police horse but did not attend any more violent marches or demonstrations. Tiff was grateful that Toby did not seem to be affected. But she knew it was a risk that all officers and horses took and a truly painful price they paid for their service.

CHAPTER 33

Wahoo

The Cronulla riots had been a dark event in Australia's history, a terrifying example of what can happen if hatred and violence are unleashed and run unchecked. It also provided a dramatic return to duties for Tiff after her maternity break.

All of the feel-good, cheerful baby emotions that Tiff had been enjoying for the past six months suddenly came to a screaming halt as she was confronted with the reality of this darker side of her job.

The risk, the challenge and the camaraderie. The unspoken allegiance between officers. The partnership and loyalty between the riders and their horses as they were immersed in the raw reality of life. The unfiltered, brutal, unsanitised world that most people like to pretend doesn't exist. Tiff didn't like it, but she was not the sort of person to ignore anything as ignoring it does not make it go away. Acknowledging this aspect of society and attempting to regulate it were the only ways that society could function safely. Tiff was proud to be a part of this effort, even if it was not always successful or perfect.

Tiff was also proud of Toby. Even though he had no idea of the philosophical aspects of his role, he served without question. He was patient and trustworthy and he had helped her ease back into her job when she had thought all was lost.

She always felt safe when she was riding him . . .

It was 2007. Tiff and Toby were ambling along the rows of exhibitors at the Gunnedah Field Days, enjoying the atmosphere and chatting with the public.

Until then, almost all of the horses accepted into the Mounted Police Unit had been Thoroughbreds as they fitted the rigid physical criteria exactly. There were always plenty to choose from as only a small number of horses find success in the racing industry, despite the thousands bred each year. The vast majority are too slow or have no or only minor success.

But the unit had recently changed from sourcing its horses from donations to being allocated a budget each year with which to buy horses. This of course opened up the range available, although the strict criteria still applied.

On this particular day, Tiff was riding Toby and there were three other officers and horses. The three other horses had been bought by the unit for $4000, $8000 and $10,000. As the four horses and riders came around the corner of a lane, they came face to face with a massive blow-up advertising figure. The figure was attached to an air compressor that would momentarily deflate its ridiculously long arms before quickly reinflating them and tossing them wildly into the air.

Suddenly there were only two horses and riders as the ten-thousand-dollar horse and the eight-thousand-dollar horse fled in opposite directions. Jeremy, the other officer still with Tiff, laughed and said jokingly to her, 'Ten thousand doesn't buy you much these days, does it? Parade only cost four thousand—he's still here and they're both gone.'

No sooner had the words left his mouth than Parade decided that the strange creature throwing its arms around was obviously not to be trusted and also bolted.

Tiffany laughed and called out to Jeremy, 'Yeah, and this one was a hundred and fifty dollars.'

By the end of 2007, Toby was considered one of the senior horses in the troop and started accompanying younger, less experienced horses on the beat. His role was to provide a calming influence in stressful situations and to take the roadside position, shielding the other horse and rider from traffic.

One night, Toby and Tiff were on patrol at the Sydney Football Stadium with Wahoo and his rider, Kelly. Wahoo had only been in the job for six months and was still a bit green, although he seemed to be progressing well. They were making their way home after directing the crowds leaving the stadium, when they came to a gate. Toby and Tiff went through first, but Wahoo refused and began to get agitated. A moment later Toby jumped sideways, and Tiffany felt an excruciating pain shoot up her leg. Wahoo had bucked and kicked out, catching Tiff in the leg just below the knee. Luckily, Kelly remained seated and managed to regain control of Wahoo as Tiff was in no state to give chase and recover a runaway horse. She had instinctively pulled her leg up in pain and now she couldn't move it. She looked down and instantly knew it was fractured. She also knew that there was no other alternative but to ride back to the stables.

So they began the slow and agonising journey back, and more than once Tiffany thanked God for Toby, who didn't react to her repeated cries of pain and remained settled and focused. He even seemed to sense she was injured and walked slowly and carefully. They were about ten minutes away from the stables, but it seemed like ten hours. By the time they got there, Tiff had managed to get herself together and think logically about a few things. First and foremost was the fact that the hospital would most likely cut off her jodhpurs and this was simply not acceptable. They were her favourite pair and she was determined to keep them. When they got back, she found a bench seat and slid off Toby and onto her good leg. The grooms took Toby back to his stable for a well-deserved clean-up and feed. A few of the other officers then brought her an office chair with wheels and wheeled her back to the change rooms. There she instructed them to carefully slip off her boots and slowly slide her jodhpurs down over her feet. It was incredibly painful, but in her eyes it was worth it. She then put on a pair of tracksuit pants and considered leaving for the hospital but realised that she was starving. It had been six hours since she had eaten and she knew that she would be sitting in a hospital emergency waiting room for at least another six, so she instructed her colleagues to wheel her up to the tearoom. Once there, they cooked up a meal and had a chat about what had happened and what would now happen.

Tiff knew she'd be off work for a while and so she made them promise to take good care of Toby. She wasn't worried about leaving him because he had coped so well while she had been on maternity leave, but she was still going to miss him. She was so thankful to him, as the thought of trying to ride any other horse for ten minutes with a fractured leg was just too awful.

After Tiff's leg was treated, she returned home to Bilpin, wondering how she would cope with this latest setback. It wasn't easy for her not to be at the unit, out on patrol every day, and this time she had an eighteen-month-old toddler to care for. One thing that was in her favour was that it was her left leg that was fractured and so she could still drive an automatic car. The first couple of days were uncomfortable but she soon adapted and was managing okay. Yet, at her check-up at the hospital about a week later, they discovered that she had a blood clot in her leg. Another one appeared a few weeks later.

Before long the fractured leg began to pale into insignificance as concern about the clots increased. Tiff began to get alarmed. There were regular doctor's visits and scans, and she started on a course of warfarin, which lasted six months. Thankfully the clots dissolved, and life eventually returned to normal.

Tiff had never imagined that she would be injured while riding Toby, but she had been in the job long enough to know that freak things did happen. She also knew that there was nothing he had done or could have done to prevent it.

For Wahoo, however, the incident at the breakaway was just the beginning.

Two years after Tiff fractured her leg, Wahoo was on patrol when he stepped backwards onto a steel grate and fell through. His rider was unharmed, but Wahoo had to have several operations to fix the bone fractures that he suffered.

Everything seemed to be going well until June 2010 when he lashed out at another horse while in his box. The horses were having their dinner, and jealousy and bad behaviour often arise at feed time. The boxes have barriers between them to stop the horses fighting but, as Wahoo lunged forwards, he knocked his eye on a clip that holds the barrier in place. It was a freak thing to occur—no horse had ever injured itself on these clips. The night guard noticed Wahoo's eye had been completely dislodged and rang the vet immediately. That night Wahoo had surgery to remove the eye, which was a success, but sadly he developed meningitis. Despite aggressive treatment, his condition worsened until finally the decision was made to euthanise him and end his suffering.

It was a tragic end for a relatively young horse who had served the community bravely for four years.

CHAPTER 34

The horse flu

Motherhood suited Tiff. Young at heart herself, she could easily relate to Bree and loved spending time with her. By the age of two Bree had her own pony and she and her mum would go riding together around the property or on the many bush trails that led off it. Tiff would lead Bree's pony off one of her own horses—usually Bundy, who she was still eventing. Bree showed no fear, sitting rock solid in a tiny stock saddle, taking in the beautiful mountain scenery as it passed her by. Tiff wasn't surprised. Like she had already realised, Bree had been riding since before she was born.

Despite the challenges of parenting, Tiff was keen to have another baby and she didn't want to leave too much of a gap between Bree and her brother or sister. But she had another significant event looming on the calendar for work and this time she didn't want to miss out.

In September 2007, Sydney would play host to the APEC (Asia-Pacific Economic Cooperation) forum. It was to be attended by 21 world leaders, including United States President George W. Bush, Russian President Vladimir Putin and the General Secretary of the Chinese Communist Party, Hu Jintao.

Thousands of police were rostered onto the APEC security operations and Sydney's central business district was cut in half by a 2.8-metre (9-feet) concrete and wire security fence. At the time, anti-Iraq war sentiment was running high and peaceful protests against President Bush were planned for the city. The Mounted Police Unit was to play a pivotal role in providing security for the event as well as providing ceremonial escorts for the leaders.

Tiff had known about this for several years and decided to put off having her second baby until after it was over. She had already missed the Military Tattoo because of pregnancy and was determined for it to not happen again. This was going to be something she would remember for years to come, one of the highlights of the ceremonial side of her career, and she couldn't believe she was going to be so close to all these world leaders.

The unit had trained and was in peak condition. Everything was ready to go, when in August, only a few weeks before the forum, there was an outbreak of equine influenza—or EI as it was known. This was the first time EI had appeared in Australia. Although it can be fatal to young foals and debilitated horses, it rarely kills adults. But recovery can take up to six months for severely affected horses and it is also highly contagious. Obviously, the Thoroughbred industry and the government stood to lose billions of dollars in gambling revenue, so EI was a catastrophic threat. Not to mention the potential loss of new foals about to be born.

On 25 August 2007, a national standstill on the movement of horses was declared, initially for 72 hours. Federal Primary Industries Minister Senator Ian Macdonald then extended the ban on horse movement for a further seven days. As case numbers continued to grow, the New South Wales government decided to make the ban on horse movements and race meetings indefinite. A massive vaccination program also commenced, with all horses in the state being immunised.

At the police stables, six horses including Toby tested positive for the virus. Within a day or so, another two horses also returned a positive result and the entire unit of 36 police horses was quarantined. Mounted Police patrols for the APEC summit were consequently cancelled. Plans to bring in police horses from other states were also abandoned, due to the travel ban.

Toby ended up one of the sickest of those infected. It started as an elevated temperature and then quickly progressed to a loss of appetite. He then developed a harsh dry cough and a nasal discharge. For a week he battled the disease. He was sluggish and lethargic, having to be forced to take short walks to maintain his circulation. He didn't want to eat and picked at his feed. Tiff looked at him and she had flashbacks to the sickly, weak youngster that she brought home in the float that night years ago. She wondered whether his poor start in life had made him particularly susceptible to illness and she hoped that wasn't the case. Then she realised that this was the first time he'd been ill since the infection after his botched castration all those years ago.

Eventually, Toby began to feel better and started a limited exercise regime. But it was a full six weeks before he and the other horses returned to full work. Even after the last horse recovered, they remained in quarantine for a further 30 days.

It was strange after four years in the Force for Toby to not work. A few times each year the police horses were spelled on a farm on the outskirts of Sydney, but this was different. The quarantine laws that were in place meant that horses could not be moved and so Toby and the others spent the entire time at the stables at Redfern.

By March 2008 the virus was successfully contained, and Australia returned to its EI-free status. More than 10,000 horses had been infected and the cost to eradicate the disease was estimated at one billion dollars.

Tiff and her colleagues were worried about their horses and disappointed by the cancellation of their APEC forum duties, but Tiff more than anyone. She had put her personal life on hold for this and now nothing. It was actually worse than the Military Tattoo. Back then she couldn't perform because she was pregnant. This time she wasn't pregnant and she still couldn't participate. Her frustration was intense, and it was so hard not to take it personally, despite the fact that she was not the only person missing out and every single horse owner in the state had been affected.

Tiff was determined to not waste any more time and ten months later, her second child was born. Tiff and Col named their healthy baby boy Kye.

Tiff had always envisaged herself with a large family. A tribe of kids—noisy, confident, exploring the countryside, arguing, playing and learning. Wild and free, unrestrained by backyard fences or boundaries. Messy and adventurous, embodying the very essence of childhood. But sadly, her experience with gestational diabetes a second time forced her to re-evaluate. It was exhausting and exacted a toll on her body that even she found gruelling. She doubted she had the stamina to cope with it again and decided that two children were enough.

The pressure of being a working mother in a challenging and demanding role such as the Mounted Police was also a factor.

In the end, Tiff realised that she had been blessed beyond measure already. She was incredibly grateful and determined to enjoy every moment with her new baby.

CHAPTER 35

Anzac Day

Sid was gaunt, drawn and haggard. His eyes stared out from two sunken sockets. Arms once wiry were now more like wire strands. He reminded Tiff of Toby in those first terrible weeks and she was alarmed.

Ann had told her Sid had lost weight, but it was more than that. There was something very wrong.

'Nah, it's just a stomach bug. Having a bit of trouble with my food,' he said.

Tiff persisted. 'Are you eating . . . properly?'

He was guarded and evasive. He didn't want to talk.

'How's Toby?' he asked, eyes brightening for a moment, and then added, 'I bet the kids have grown. Are they up yet?'

After breakfast they went for a walk. Sid proudly showed her Clyde, brimming with life in stark contrast to himself. 'You and Col should take him out. I haven't had much energy lately. He probably needs a good stretch.'

'Sid, have you been to the doctor?'

There. She finally said it. If Sid wasn't riding, there was definitely something wrong.

He glanced at her momentarily before dropping his gaze. 'Yeah, you know, the same old stuff. I always knew it was going to kill me.'

'The grog?' inquired Tiff.

'Yeah, mind you I'd have been dead long ago without it. I suppose it gave me a stay of execution. Forty years isn't something to be sneezed at.' Then he added, 'But don't worry. I'm not going anywhere just yet.'

While she was scared and worried, Tiff was glad she'd come to visit because at least she knew what was going on. It was just as well because, like Jock's, Sid's decline came quickly.

A few weeks later, Ann rang her at work. Tiff was still in the yard, just about to go out on patrol.

'He's not good, Tiffy. I've been taking him into the hospital but he's worse. He asked me to call you. He wants to see you.'

'Of course,' Tiff answered. 'I'll be up on the weekend.'

The idea of a six-hour drive after a long working week didn't thrill her, nor did driving that distance with two children under five, but she was committed to seeing Sid and helping him in whatever way she could. Luckily Col managed to swing the weekend off work and volunteered to drive them.

They arrived late in the evening. The lights were on in Jinki, giving a warm, encouraging glow as they pulled in the driveway, but Tiff knew that glow was misleading. There was nothing warm or cheering about what was awaiting her.

They carried the sleeping children inside and put them to bed, then sat with Ann and Errol and chatted about life in general. When they had wound down, they ventured off to bed knowing that Bree and Kye would wake at the crack of dawn.

Tiff woke the next morning to Kye grizzling, standing and peering over the porta cot in the corner of the room. She swept him up and carried him to the kitchen to prepare his Weetbix and before long Bree appeared. It was about nine before the kids were settled and Tiff ventured outside. Sid wasn't up so she went to visit Clyde. She had to admit, she always felt a little in awe in Clyde's presence. He was majestic and, like Sid had mentioned, he had an aura like Toby's: 'the old soul feel about him'.

Clyde came over and she rubbed his nose up and down just like she did with Toby. He was a sweet gentle boy, expertly trained by Sid, a grandmaster of horses.

Tiff had taken Sid up on his offer last time she had been here and ridden Clyde down to the beach. It had been bliss, like something out of a dream. She was so happy that Sid had bought him and found happiness again after Jock's death.

'He's pretty special, but then you already know that, don't you?' Sid appeared silently behind her like a dandelion wisp, blown in on the breeze.

'He's gorgeous,' said Tiff. 'He's like a giant teddy bear. I just want to hug him.' When she turned to face Sid, she tried to hide her shock, but a gasp escaped her lips. He was thinner than before, if that was possible, and his skin had a sallow, yellowy glow. Even his eyeballs were yellow.

Tiff felt terrible. Sid was her friend and she wanted him to feel comfortable. After a few awkward moments, she said, 'How are you?' then instantly regretted asking such a stupid question.

Sid smiled. 'Well, I've seen better days, that's for sure.' Tiff was one of the few people he could relate to. Their love of horses had brought them together over the years and it was the reason he had asked her here today.

'It's come on a bit quicker than I expected, Tiffy. They say I don't have long, and I was wondering if you could do me a favour?'

'Of course. Anything,' said Tiff.

'Would you take care of Clyde for me?'

'Oh Sid, you don't even have to ask,' said Tiff, heartbroken.

'Actually, I was wondering,' he continued, 'do you think he'd be suited to the Mounted Police?'

'I think he'd be perfect, Sid,' she replied truthfully.

'Well, can you do what needs to be done? I'd be so proud of him if he makes it. Toby could teach him the ropes and you'd see him all the time.'

Tiff had to admit it was a great idea. When Sid first asked her, she had imagined taking Clyde back to Bilpin, but the Mounties would be an ideal life for him. And she knew his gentle disposition and the fact that he had been trained by Sid would make him an outstanding police horse, just like Toby.

Sadly, there would be no parades. No shiny nameplate on a stable door. No patrols with Toby.

A few weeks later, just as Tiff was finalising Clyde's paperwork for the Mounted Police, Ann rang one Sunday afternoon with terrible news. Clyde had fallen and broken his shoulder and had to be euthanised.

Now it was Tiff's turn to be angry with the invisible foe. There was no sense to it; nothing could justify the loss of such a beautiful horse. And poor Sid, losing the small bit of joy in his otherwise dark world. He didn't deserve this, none of it.

'Sid hasn't spoken about it. He didn't shoot him; he got Mary to put him down. That's how bad he is.'

'Should I come up?' asked Tiff.

'No, he told me to tell you not to come. He's leaving this afternoon; someone is coming to pick him up and take him up the Tablelands. Apparently, he has a family member up there and the Department of Veterans' Affairs has organised for him to be cared for in a hospice. He doesn't want to be a burden here.'

'Shit,' said Tiff.

'We've always known he needed his privacy. This is just his final request.'

'Yeah, I know,' said Tiff. 'But it's hard. I would have liked to say goodbye.'

'He told me to thank you for everything and for all the work you did getting Clyde a trial with the Mounties.'

'I can't believe Clyde's dead. He was such an incredible horse. It's so unfair.' Tiff was still in shock. But what Ann said next brought home the reality of what was about to come.

'He also said that next Anzac Day when you and Toby are marching, to look beside you. He'll be marching with you.'

Toby looked splendid in his ceremonial gear, his coat gleaming from hours of grooming, his ears keenly pricked, anticipating the excitement of a parade. The pomp and pageantry were electric; everyone was smiling, except for Tiff.

She sat astride Toby, wearing her grandfather's medals, tears streaming down her face. As they set off, it became worse. She was glad she was riding Toby as she could barely see where they were going.

Tiff had found out about a month after he left Jinki that Sid had passed. She remembered his message and looked to her left, wondering whether he was riding Jock or Clyde.

The tears began to subside as a surge of gratitude swept over her.

Gratitude to all the people who had lost their lives in war and those who survived but came home broken. People like Sid, whose whole life had been irrevocably changed at the age of twenty-one due to the brutality and the absolute futility of war.

Tiff looked to her left again and realised it was Jock. Maybe it would be Clyde's turn next year.

CHAPTER 36

Falls

It started out as the odd bit of stiffness, an aching pain or a sharp jolt like a mild electric shock. Because there was no consistency or uniformity to the pain, Tiff ignored it. Ibuprofen seemed to work, was easy to access and fast to take effect, until it wore off and the pain returned.

Tiff consoled herself with the fact that all horseriders, in fact all people with physical occupations, had the occasional bit of pain, but she was only in her mid-thirties. She shouldn't feel like this. Instead of waking refreshed, she would wake feeling like she'd been trampled on. Some days it was an effort to get through the day and six to eight hours in the saddle was torture.

People started to notice Tiff's stiffness as she dismounted. Her agonising first few steps as she fought to regain her mobility were obvious. When they asked if she was okay, she would always pass it off with a laugh. But it soon became apparent that something was seriously wrong when getting on and off the bigger horses became a problem.

After Toby had joined the unit, Tiff had ridden him religiously until she went on maternity leave with Bree. He had nursed and supported her back into the job she loved. So much so that after she returned from leave, she started to ride other horses. As much as she wanted to be paired with him, she knew she had to be fair. Other people needed him more.

Over the following years, as Tiff's experience increased, she took on an increasing number of young, less experienced horses. Eventually she moved into a training role.

It was ironic. After all they had been through, she and Toby were growing apart because of their skills. Her skill in training horses and Toby's in training riders.

Training the young, green recruits was incredibly rewarding but it also came with drawbacks. Sitting astride a 500-kilogram animal with a mind of its own, no matter how quiet or trustworthy, is always fraught with risk. Add to that their youth and inexperience in a highly stimulating environment, and falls can almost be guaranteed.

Often it wasn't the fault of the horse at all. Horses can trip and go down. In a paddock or sand arena, this is usually not a major problem but on a hard surface such as a road, the consequences can be serious or even fatal. Tiff had had a number of these falls and in her younger days she always bounced back, but even relatively minor tumbles were now taking their toll.

When she factored in the major accidents that she had suffered over the years, it was becoming increasingly apparent why her body was breaking down. There had been the accident at the Easter Show in 2003. There had been the fractured leg and blood clots from Wahoo at Moore Park in 2007. There had even been one earlier in the week. She had been out on patrol when a car almost collided with other cars and she and her horse had to jump sideways to avoid being hit. She fell off and hit the road and was momentarily stunned but otherwise okay. As per policy, Tiff was taken to hospital to be assessed and given a few days to recuperate. The doctor who attended her at St Vincent's was a lovely young intern who was thorough and thoughtful.

Less than a week later she was back there, this time nursing a broken leg. He looked at her in disbelief and said, 'You are the second Mounted Police Officer I've treated this week.' Tiff laughed when she realised he didn't recognise her and replied, 'I know, I was the other officer.'

Then in 2009, there was Centennial Park.

It had been a Wednesday, a training day. These days were usually great fun. The officers would take the horses over to the park and train them in various activities or, if an exhibition was approaching, practise their musical ride. On this particular day, it was a general training day. The horses were doing various exercises to learn teamwork and how to work in pairs.

Tiff was riding Ismo, a young horse. The activity called for them to form pairs and then canter or gallop along in a straight line holding a piece of rope between them. They had done it a few times before and Ismo was starting to understand what was expected of him. He was a lovely, big horse and Tiff had no doubt that he would make a fine police horse. But on their final attempt, the other horse farted. It wasn't a discreet, inconspicuous fart (horses don't do discreet farts); it was loud and boisterous. In such proximity, it was simply too much for Ismo to bear.

He reacted violently. To Tiff, it was as though someone had detonated a fuse. She could actually feel him recoil underneath her and she knew what was coming. He was in a full gallop. She knew he had the momentum to do something truly terrifying and she was right.

Ismo wrenched the reins from her and exploded, and yet again she experienced the slow-motion series of bucks that increased in force until she was flying through the air and headed for the ground.

Once again, there was just blackness. Tiff remembered nothing about the day and, for a while afterwards, not even what had happened. She woke in hospital with a cervical collar and severe bruising to her back and right hip. She had trouble walking and even moving.

Looking back, that was it: the fall that ended Tiff's career.

Initially Tiff rallied, thinking that she was too young and too invested to give up yet. She also believed that with some medical intervention it could all be fixed.

She was wrong.

Tiff was diagnosed with tendonitis in her hip, not only from the numerous falls but also from the repetitive strain of riding. In addition to that she had several severely damaged discs, which only added to her hip problems.

Tiff began a long process of treatments, including rest, exercise physiology, cortisone injections and physiotherapy. Despite all this she continued to go backwards. After a few hours in the saddle, it was as though her spine and hips were fused and then at night they would ache. Painkillers no longer worked.

Eventually there was no other option than to go on restricted duties.

It was a confusing time. Here Tiff was, at the height of her career, sharing it with the horse of her dreams. But now she was having to take a step back and accept that maybe things were not going to turn out as she had thought they would.

That maybe life had other plans for her.

CHAPTER 37

The Military Tattoo 2010

There was one thing Tiff was not going to concede and that
was the 2010 Edinburgh Military Tattoo.

After the disappointment of the 2005 event and then
APEC in 2007, Tiff was convinced that the highlights of the
decade had passed her by. Then, unbelievably, she learned that
due to the success of the 2005 Tattoo (perhaps minus Toby's
blunder) it was returning to Australia in 2010 to perform four
shows. The New South Wales Mounted Police and the Police
Band were invited to perform again.

A lot can happen in five years. Children learn to speak,
walk and develop their own personalities.

In five years, Toby too had learned and grown. He was
no longer a novice. He no longer fretted when Tiff was not
there. He was now strong, confident and dependable.

Five years after his spectacular bomb at the 2005 event, Toby was selected as one of sixteen horses to return to Aussie Stadium and perform again.

Not only that but he was also considered one of the four best horses of the Mounted unit and assigned the role of a rear section leader. This was a critical role because when the troop split into four for different formations, the section leaders initiated the divergence and then set the pace in preparation for the merging of the group once again. Their timing, speed and skill were key to the success of the performance.

This time, there was no doubt in anyone's mind that Toby could do it. He had performed the ride countless times over the years, all of them faultlessly, and had been one of the senior horses of the unit for more than three years. Best of all, Tiff would be riding him.

Under a starlit February night, the unit waited excitedly, sixteen horses and riders about to enter a stadium in front of a crowd of thousands and a TV audience of millions.

The lights were blinding, and it took a few moments for Tiff's eyes to adjust. Millions of tiny insects swarmed in clouds around the lights, drawn by their brilliance and heat.

The ambience was like nothing Tiff had ever encountered before. There was a palpable feeling of anticipation. People expected to be wowed; they came to be enthralled. And with that came initial feelings of apprehension, yet at the same time a confidence she had never known.

The noise varied from deafening roars to moments of spellbound silence and in between there was the general chatter of tens of thousands of people and the announcer's voice reverberating around the stadium.

But all this stopped as Toby and Tiff stepped into the arena. Suddenly there were no lights, no sounds, no scents or feels. There was just a horse and his rider, coming together as one.

Their remarkable ten-year journey flashed through her mind, culminating in this extraordinary event. The neglected, rescued horse with a face only a mother could love standing with the woman who saved him. The same horse, now proud and courageous, standing with the same woman whose courage he had restored. They had come full circle and tonight was their ultimate celebration.

Then as they moved out into the arena, Toby and Tiff became four.

It felt like an invisible elastic thread appeared and bonded the three other horses in her section to her and Toby. It held them together so they could perform in a line and then separate and rejoin seamlessly. It made the four individual horses and riders one component, one quarter of the magical whole.

Each of the four sections became like a coloured thread weaving an intricate pattern as they flew around the arena. The Police Band music was so ingrained, the moves so well

257

rehearsed, their intuition and instinct so strong, it was no wonder they delivered a faultless performance.

For eight minutes they danced, weaving their different threads into a living tapestry for all to see. A testament to the infinite beauty of the bond between horse and human. A tribute to the trust, faith and love between these incredible animals and their devoted partners.

Then it was over and reluctantly Tiff returned to earth. The adrenalin was still pumping, her heart was still racing, and her legs were like jelly. She knew that nothing would ever compare to this. Toby was equally euphoric and, just as she had predicted, no one noticed that ungainly head, the freckled face or spotty nose. He was Toby the magnificent.

After the show, members of the public walked through the temporary stables and Tiff was delighted when people told her how beautiful he was and asked, 'Was he a racehorse?' She swore Toby inflated his chest and grew in height every time this question was asked. She had no doubt that he understood every word.

It had been an amazing experience and Tiff was thankful to have been able to do it. She soaked up every second, recording it in her brain for later because she knew that moments like these were limited, as was her time as a Mounted Police Officer.

CHAPTER 38

Restricted duties

'Restricted' was not a word in Tiff's vocabulary. Lively, active, energetic, yes. Determined, fearless—definitely. Restricted, no.

It came as no surprise then that restricted duties was a bitter pill to swallow. Reduced riding hours meant her time had to be taken up doing other things, so Tiff found herself performing admin, public relations and cleaning tack again.

Fortunately, a new role became available, one that she enjoyed tremendously and was very good at: she was tasked with buying potential police horses and rehoming the retiring ones. She had always loved buying and selling things but now she got to do it with horses *and* someone else's money. It was almost too good to be true.

259

Tiff was a bit surprised that they let her take on the role, especially considering her first experience as a police horse buyer a few years back had been somewhat unconventional.

It was 2006. Tiff was in Scone for the annual Scone Horse Festival with Toby and another officer, Karen. It was great for them all to escape the city and spend a few days in the country. They even led the parade up the main street of town.

There were numerous events over the ten days of the festival but the one that captured Tiff's attention most was the Stockman's Challenge. This is a gruelling competition that is designed to commemorate Australian riders' horse skills. While she was impressed with the skill of the riders, it was the horses that she noticed most. They were incredible. Absolutely bomb-proof. Their riders were cracking stock-whips while hanging off the side of them. There was noise, people, chaos—and these horses never batted an eyelid. They were coping with everything that a fully fledged police horse had to deal with.

Karen was responsible for buying new horses, but Tiff was interested and keen to be involved in the process.

'What do you think of these horses? Do you think they'd be suitable for police work?' she asked Karen, who shrugged and replied, 'Yeah I suppose so; they're pretty quiet.'

'I might just go and have a chat with their owners,' said Tiff.

'Are you kidding me?' Karen called after her, but it was too late.

Tiff and Toby trotted over to a group of stockmen, who immediately took on a defensive pose. She was used to this, unfortunately. There was silence as she pulled Toby to a halt. She looked around and tried to start a conversation.

'Great work out there, boys.'

She was met with silence until one of the riders spoke up awkwardly and said, 'Thanks.'

They looked at her expectantly, waiting for her to clarify what she was really doing there, so she decided to put them out of their discomfort and explain.

'So . . . the Mounted Police need some more horses for some big events that are coming up.'

'Like what?' asked someone.

'Well, there is the APEC forum and World Youth Day.'

Again she was met with silence and she could see that these names meant nothing to them.

'So,' she explained, 'the Mounted Police Unit is providing escort and protection to all of these VIPs, and we need to train more horses in a short time. Normally we like to take on young horses, but at the moment we're looking for older horses who already have many of the skills we are looking for.'

'So you think our horses might be good for that?' someone asked a bit disbelievingly.

'Yeah, I do,' she answered.

Nobody knew what to say. By this stage, there was quite a crowd around Tiff and Toby as more and more people wondered who was 'in trouble'.

Finally, in an attempt to get some interest in her cause, she casually added, 'We will pay up to ten thousand dollars for the right horse.'

The reaction was instant; people who only a few seconds before had been about to walk away were now pushing to get to the front to talk to her. People started shouting over the top of each other. Even Toby pricked up his ears.

Tiff ended up talking to a group of seriously interested stockmen for about half an hour and narrowed it down to one horse who sounded almost too good to be true. He was ten years old. A little bit older than usual, but in this case, the unit was happy to take on older horses as it meant they could shortcut the training and desensitisation process. His name was Doctor and he had been a performance and circus horse. There was nothing that he hadn't seen or done, and Tiff was thrilled. She told Karen about him, who suggested Tiff follow it up, seeing as she had found him. This was exactly what Tiff was hoping she'd say, as she was keen to show what she could do.

A few days later when the negotiations were complete, she hooked up the police float and headed out towards Mudgee. It was actually out of Mudgee, but the guy had given her a great set of instructions. It was in the days before GPS, so she was relying on these instructions as well as some detailed maps.

She'd written it down. 'Go about 20 km out of town, then turn right just past the giant dead tree on your left. Go past the cattle yards and then swing right again. Go down the road for about 15 km and you'll see a burnt-out old car. Hang a left there and continue till you see a blue house set back from the road. There's a track about 100 metres on from that, on your left. Go slow or you'll miss it. Go down there, then up the hills (there're a couple). Keep going till you get to the top and then go to the left at the set of gates. When you get to the yards, beep, and I'll come and meet you.'

It all sounded pretty clear and, even if it wasn't, Tiff was too excited to care anyway.

Tiff followed the directions to a tee. Everything that the guy had said was there. Except for the hills. The 'hills' were in fact a mountain and the track was a goat track. A dusty, treacherous, narrow cutting on the side of a steep mountain. The moment she started driving up it, she realised she was in trouble. The track got narrower and steeper, and the traction got worse. Tiff was already 'leaning forward' in the driver's seat in a futile attempt to help the car and float navigate the incline but it was to no avail. The car started revving dangerously and she was already in first gear.

The float started moving sideways. Eventually she stopped. She knew it wasn't the ideal thing to do but otherwise she risked losing the float over the side of the mountain, and it would drag the car and her with it. Realising she was well and truly stuck, she was about to ring the unit and explain what had happened.

Suddenly she heard a noise behind her. At first, she thought she was imagining it, but she wound the window down and, sure enough, it was the noise of a vehicle coming up the road. She couldn't work out what it was—it definitely wasn't a car. Then in her rear-vision mirror, she saw a tractor, and she remembered the farmer who had been slashing his paddock alongside the track she turned down. He had raised his hand to her in greeting then looked a bit shocked when she turned down the track, but she hadn't thought anything of it. She had waved back enthusiastically. It was nice when people waved. Sometimes people were happy to see the police float; sometimes they weren't.

Obviously, he'd had grave concerns about her ability to make it to the top and decided to follow her. She jumped out of the car and went to meet him. He was a man of few words. He surveyed the situation and quickly hooked up a chain to the front of her vehicle and proceeded to pull her up the slope and onto more even ground. He assured her that she would be fine to make the rest of the journey. He knew exactly where she was going—there was only one property at the top of the mountain.

Tiff thanked him and continued. Finally, she made it to the top, pulled up alongside some yards, and tooted her horn. A few minutes later the guy from Scone appeared and took her to see Doctor.

Tiff looked at the beautiful bay gelding and she felt the earth collapse beneath her. He was lucky if he was 15.1 hands. The height requirement right there and then was blown. She turned to the owner.

'I told you they have to be 16 hands.'

'Did you? Oh, I don't remember that.'

Tiff stood for the second time in the past hour and thought, 'What the hell do I do now?' Buying horses was a hell of a lot more complicated than she had imagined.

She looked at Doctor and thought that seeing she'd travelled all this way, she may as well see what he could do. For the next hour she rode him, and he met every challenge she put to him. He was kind, unflappable and intelligent. Just the damn height was against him. In the heat of the moment, she decided that after all she had been through, and knowing how good this horse actually was, she would take a chance and buy him. To hell with his height.

She loaded him up and left the property. The trip down the mountain, although stressful, was at least without incident. But Tiff was stressed all the same. How was she going to explain her purchase? She realised that she needed to at least prepare Karen for the inevitable, so she rang her from just outside Lithgow.

'So, you bought him. How is he?' she asked.

'He's great, amazing actually. He's just a little . . . small.'

'What? How small?' asked Karen.

'I don't know—I didn't have a measuring stick with me,' said Tiff, knowing full well how small he was.

Then miraculously the call dropped out and Tiff drove the rest of the way to the stables a little more at ease.

Of course, when Tiff arrived in Redfern, she had to face the music but, unlike Toby's debut, Doctor didn't break anyone's arm. He was perfect and wowed everyone with his calm and relaxed manner. Everyone agreed that he would be a valuable asset to the unit as long as he was used for the smaller riders. With APEC and World Youth Day fast approaching, they needed good horses and really couldn't afford to be picky.

So, while the whole venture had been a success on the surface, behind the scenes it had been a debacle. Tiff still wasn't sure how she had managed to pull it off but, like so many things in her life, she just thanked the universe and ploughed on regardless.

Which is where Tiff found herself now. The official buyer for the Mounted Police Unit. It was a huge responsibility but Tiff had no doubts. She was confident in her judgement, and she knew she had a good eye for horses. She just had to pay some attention to the requirements.

Even more than a decade ago when she saw a half-dead horse taking refuge from the unrelenting heat under a scant sapling, she had known . . .

CHAPTER 39

Leaving the Mounted Police

The doctor said nothing. He did a few tests and wrote down some notes. Tiff felt awkward. She was trying to be chatty and friendly, yet he responded in monosyllables. Finally she stopped talking and looked out the window.

He looked at her over the rim of his glasses. 'You're a lot worse, aren't you?' It was a statement rather than a question.

'Uh-huh,' said Tiff, feeling uncomfortable.

It was true. The travel from Bilpin to Redfern was taking its toll. Sitting in a car for up to four hours a day was having a similar impact on her body to riding. All of her muscles and tendons were contracting, and she was in more and more pain. She couldn't believe that even after giving up so much she was still suffering, and knew in the back of her mind that her days were numbered.

The doctor was blunt and detached. He explained that the driving was exacerbating her injuries and marked on her file that she was not to drive for more than 45 minutes at a time. Effective immediately.

That was it. In the stroke of a pen, a career that had taken years to attain and spanned nearly thirteen years was over.

It was a fifteen-minute drive but in peak-hour traffic it took thirty and when Tiff pulled up at the stables, she could remember none of it. She walked into the office and stood there, dazed. She glanced around, thinking about her first day and all of the days since then.

Tiff realised that she had learned more than she had ever thought possible about people, horses and herself. She had grown in confidence and wisdom but sacrificed her health in the process.

This was not just an ordinary job, and her workmates were not just ordinary colleagues. They were like family. A loud, raucous extended family where everyone looked out for each other. Where people knew when to leave you alone and give you space and when you needed a helping hand.

And now Tiff was leaving. She knew she could always visit them, but it would never be the same. Then she thought of the horses. How could she leave them, leave Toby?

Tiff's news was greeted with shock and disbelief. Pretty much the same emotions she was feeling. Everyone was crying, especially some of the grooms with whom she had a great relationship. It was so sudden, so unexpected, so final.

Tiff made her way down the walkway of the stable block and said goodbye to all of the horses. The horses who had taught her so much and the horses who had broken her body. They were all a part of her story and would hold a special place in her heart.

She did not say goodbye to Toby. That was not possible, nor was it necessary. He would always be with her. They would just be apart for a while.

Then Tiff walked out through the historic gates for the last time. She didn't look back. She climbed into her car and began the long drive home. It was a lot longer than 45 minutes but she didn't care.

Tiff began the grieving process. She felt anger and loss then finally acceptance. Once the shock cleared and she could think more objectively, she realised that it was inevitable. She had tried everything to alleviate the pain and lessen the discomfort, but nothing had worked. She tried to look on the bright side. At least if she had to work closer to home, she would be able to spend more time with her children.

Tiff applied for a transfer to the closest police station to home, which coincidentally was where Col worked. She was still a member of the Mounted Police but split her time on restricted duties with the Windsor station.

It was strange to be back working with Col. By now he was a Sergeant and she was a Leading Senior Constable.

A few years previously, the Force had introduced 'Leading' as a position between Senior Constable and Sergeant. It acknowledged those officers who took on a training role. In the General side of policing, these were the Senior Constables who trained the Probationary Constables and the recruits from the Police Academy. In the Mounted Police, it was assumed that there was no need to use the title 'Leading' as everyone who entered the unit had completed three years of general duties. But it was common knowledge that there was a long and rigorous training process that all Mounted Police undertook when they first joined and that senior officers were invaluable in providing that training and support. Over the years Tiff had helped induct and train many of the new recruits, as well as the horses, and so eventually when three Leading Senior Constable positions were allocated to the unit, she applied for one and was successful.

Tiff was proud of her achievements, especially considering— like so many women—she had managed to do this while dealing with two difficult pregnancies and then raising a family.

Tiff's new life was a huge adjustment after thirteen years as a Mounted Policewoman. She was largely deskbound as she was not able to perform the range of duties required by a police officer on patrol, so she mainly handled warrants and summons. She was still the official buyer for the Mounted Police Unit and responsible for checking on any police horses that were being spelled at Colo, near the Windsor police station. She made an effort to be happy but she mourned her previous life, the people, the horses— and Toby.

Tiff had known she would have trouble disconnecting from him and she was right. Even though one of the other riders, Nadia, was besotted with him, Tiff couldn't help feeling like she had abandoned him. She rang the unit regularly like an obsessed parent and wasn't sure whether she should be pleased or disappointed that he seemed to be coping okay. She consoled herself that he would retire back into her care when the time came but she still missed him like crazy.

Tiff reasoned that she had spent more time with Toby in the past twelve years than many people do with their partner in a relationship, so it was perfectly normal that she would feel this way. But on a deeper level, she knew that it was more than this. Something that she would never understand or explain. It was as though they had formed a connection, a link, when she found him all those years ago. Now they were joined in some sort of cosmic partnership.

She knew, though, that while her life of duty had come to an end, his was still active and she had to respect that.

In February 2014, Tiff officially retired from the New South Wales Police Force.

Her sixteen years of service had changed her in many ways. Before she joined the Force, she had never noticed people's faces. They were just incidental to the conversation she was engaged in. But now, she knew this was the one thing she would never forget.

The crimson-faced fury of the drunk as he repeatedly punched her.

The accident victims, scared, nervous and traumatised.

The vacant, blank-faced stare of the battered victim.

The life force draining from a person's face as they took their last breath.

And the wide-eyed wonder of the children and adults as they stepped forwards to pat Toby and experience the magic of interacting with a 600-kilo gentle giant. Their questions, their joy, their pure delight made the unbearable bearable and everything worthwhile.

Tiff's career had been raw and at times brutal but it was authentic and she felt incredibly grateful and honoured to have served.

Now at the age of forty she was about to take a step forwards into a new world, a foreign world which, unlike the Police Force, had no rules, regulations or routine.

It was a giant leap of faith. Luckily Tiff was used to taking giant leaps.

CHAPTER 40

Nadia

While Toby's early life had been undeniably cruel, since then he almost appeared to have been blessed with good fortune. After Tiff retired, for a time it seemed like he was on his own, but it was not long before another officer fell completely in love with him.

Nadia joined the Police Force in 2009. She transferred into the Mounted unit in 2014, not long after Tiff moved to Windsor. At that time Toby was predominantly being ridden by two riders, Sarah and Trevor. As he was often used for new officers, he was then allocated to Nadia.

The attraction was instant. While the others joked about his appearance, all she could see was his beauty. Like Tiff and Sid before her, she had seen into his soul, and it would change her forever. Even after she was inducted, Toby was listed as her preferred mount and she rode him almost exclusively.

Nadia felt like a halo of white light surrounded her when she rode Toby. She was safe and secure, and she trusted him with her life. And just like a human police partner, she knew they 'had each other's back'.

Nadia's care of Toby extended far beyond that of just a rider. She loved grooming him and spending time with him after they had returned to the stables. The horses are always hosed down and walked for twenty minutes to make sure their feet are completely dry before they are put away into their stable. The shavings that are used for bedding can get trapped in the gaps between their shoes and the soles of their feet, and if they are still wet it can cause foot problems. This walk is a social time for officers, grooms and horses. Many a cheerful conversation takes place as they amble along the historic cobblestones of the precinct. Sometimes they will stop for a while and chat. Toby always used this opportunity to have a mutual back scratch with whatever horses were also being walked.

Back scratching is actually a grooming behaviour. The horse uses its teeth to scrape and scratch the other horse, typically along the backbone and neck, places where they can't reach themselves. They are usually very careful but occasionally a horse may become a little overzealous and unintentionally nip the other. The transgression will always be acknowledged with a high-pitched indignant squeal, but normally all will be forgiven and they will start up again within a few moments.

Many horses enjoy back scratching, but no other horse came close to Toby's level of enthusiasm. He simply adored it and many times Nadia would have to drag his 600-kilo frame reluctantly away.

She also loved to 'pretty' him up.

Just before her first Easter Show and musical ride she brought in some horse make-up and gave him a makeover. Horse make-up is similar to human make-up. It covers blemishes and highlights the eyes. Nadia was thrilled when everyone in the unit agreed that Toby had never looked so good. Toby of course didn't care. He was comfortable in his own skin.

It was just as well Toby didn't care because this was just the start. On Halloween Nadia adorned him with glowing pumpkins. At Christmas time it was a Santa hat and a Rudolf nose. Even when he was trying to have a quiet snooze in his stable, she decorated him with a hat and glasses like the old man that he was.

Toby never even had a chance to miss Tiff when he had such an adoring replacement.

Over the years Toby and Nadia shared many memorable moments. She rode Toby at the front of the Guard of Honour for the funeral for Bev Moroney, wife of the former Police Commissioner and long-time supporter of the Mounted Police Unit. Then in 2014 they led the White Ribbon March in Sydney in support of domestic violence victims. They also had the honour of leading Aboriginal soldiers in the Sydney Anzac Day march. Toby seemed to absorb the intensity of these events and always appeared serious and thoughtful, far removed from his usual cheerful, even goofy, self.

Nadia was overjoyed that Toby was given such a high profile at these ceremonial events. Over the years the Mounted unit had not only accepted Toby's looks but had even begun to celebrate them. Out of all the grand, beautiful horses they had to call on, it seemed that Toby had become their unofficial mascot. No matter where they went—rain, hail or shine—Toby's face would always be front and centre of the local country daily, city newspaper or evening news. So much so that it became a running joke within the unit. It was as though his face was so compelling that photographers zeroed in on him wherever he went. Troop horse Toby had become Toby the poster boy.

Nadia, of course, couldn't have been prouder. But while these ceremonial duties were rousing, it was the everyday general policing duties that made her feel most at home with Toby. The two of them plodding along through the streets of Sydney or a country town, interacting with the public.

Whether it was making their way up narrow, claustro-phobic passageways in Martin Place, riding under carports in Mount Druitt or walking up sandstone stairs in Surry Hills, there was nowhere Toby wouldn't go. No matter what Nadia asked of him, he did it unquestioningly.

Toby also delighted people with his ability to navigate gates and stairs and poke his head in the front door of the houses of some of his inner-city admirers.

He was a hit with the kids at 'schoolies' at Tweed Heads. His beautiful nature and calming presence broke down barriers and allowed Nadia to relate to the teenagers on a personal level rather than as a law enforcer, making them far more receptive to her presence and directions.

Even when they were involved in a highly charged, dangerous crowd surge one New Year's Eve, Toby never lost his cool. He carried Nadia safely, despite being hit across the hindquarters by a drunken member of the public. There was no reaction, no retaliation; Toby just continued per-forming the job he had been sent to do, ensuring the safety of the thousands of people who had flocked to the city to enjoy the occasion.

Nadia was astounded by the depth of her feeling for Toby. Before long she was aware that she was hopelessly, totally and utterly in love with him.

As the years wore on, she began to refer to him as Manny, after the caring, fatherly mammoth in the *Ice Age* movies.

It was a term of endearment, a name that captured the essence of Toby, her own protective gentle giant.

Nadia began to wonder how she could ever cope without him.

CHAPTER 41

History repeats

Three years after Tiff left the Mounties, Toby also began to show signs that he was not completely sound. At first, it seemed minor. A bit of stiffness, a little swelling. After a few days rest, he would be right. But then it would recur.

By this time, Toby had become an indispensable part of the unit. He could be sent to any job, whether it was routine, ceremonial or high risk. His level head and calm disposition were counted on time and time again.

This was why the gradual deterioration in his condition was such a shock. Many police horses serve well into their twenties. Toby was only fifteen.

But Toby was a Clydesdale-cross and Tiff had noticed that they seemed to show a propensity for a condition called ringbone. In fact, Bundy had recently been retired from competition after being diagnosed with both ringbone and a similar condition, sidebone.

Ringbone is a type of osteoarthritis that affects the coffin or pastern joint of a horse. It is characterised by bony growths around the joint and causes first discomfort then pain and lameness. It was the first thing that was investigated through X-ray but luckily Toby's result came back negative.

Toby was then sent for some R&R at the spelling farm at Upper Colo and came back normal. Everyone hoped that that was all he needed but, within a few months, the swelling began to reappear. He went on leave again and returned but the swelling appeared again, more quickly this time. It was now localised at the back of his fetlock. Eventually Toby was diagnosed with wind puffs, which are synovial fluid-filled swellings of the tendon sheath. While these often don't cause discomfort, in Toby's case they obviously did and could have been a precursor to a more serious problem if left to progress.

It was becoming obvious that, as with Tiff only a few years before, Toby's time was going to be cut short. While the police horses receive only the best of care, the physical demands on them are immense. When they are working, they are ridden four to six hours a day, often on hard surfaces such as roads.

If a horse is not completely sound, the repetition and work can exacerbate their condition until it becomes more and more severe. Tiff knew that the decision to retire Toby would have to be made soon. She didn't want to see him permanently lamed, but at the same time she wanted him to stay in the job he loved for as long as he could. She knew he would miss so many aspects of his life in the unit.

Toby was a police horse as surely as if he had been born into the role. He seemed to love the routine, the busyness, the adoration from the public and the company of other horses. But he was always an individual. Tiff smiled when she thought about all the things that made him unique. His swagger in time to music, his appetite for banana peels, the escaping from his stable to go to have a roll, and of course that face. That big, ungainly, motley face. He certainly was a smorgasbord of eccentricity. Toby wasn't the only one who would find his departure hard—there were also the many people who loved and depended on him.

Finally, in mid-2016, Tiff made the arrangements to bring him to his new home.

Tiff arrived at the police stables on a cloudy Tuesday morning and parked her float in the laneway. People had been saying goodbye to Toby for a couple of days but there was still a crowd gathered to pay their respects. It was clear that he would be greatly missed and never forgotten.

For Nadia, it was a blow. She couldn't imagine life without Toby, although she didn't want to see him permanently lamed either. She had hoped and prayed for months that his lameness could be fixed and was broken-hearted when it wasn't. She was inconsolable the morning of his departure, so much so that her colleagues went to great pains to stress the fact that his retirement was actually a good thing for him and that he wasn't dying. Tiff also reassured her that she would always be welcome to visit him at Bilpin.

Nadia was the last person to say goodbye to Toby before he was put in the float. She kissed his face and told him he would always be her sweet Manny.

Tiff was humbled by the reaction of all these people who loved him. She thought back to Gary's words, 'Well, look at him—who would want that? It's a waste of money feeding him.'

How wrong that man had been in so many respects. Toby had met every challenge in his life with bravery, acceptance and trust. He was kind, honest and loyal and in a few short years had risen to the top in one of the most demanding and prestigious roles a horse can have.

Tiff led Toby up into the float. He had no idea that he was leaving for good. That a new life awaited him, just like it had for Tiff when she walked through these gates four years earlier. He simply followed her trustingly, like he would if she was leading him to the end of the earth.

Tiff wanted to tell Toby that he should be proud, that he had done what most *people* could only ever dream of doing. That he had served his community and state with dedication and courage. That he was everything and more than what she had ever imagined. More than anything she wanted to tell him that she was so glad she'd gone back that day and given him a second chance.

Toby had changed her life and the lives of so many people forever. He was, quite simply, an inspiration.

Instead, she patted his neck and said, 'So I wonder what the future holds for two worn-out old coppers?'

Toby turned to look at her, his face showing no fear, just interest and anticipation for the next adventure that awaited them. And in that instant, Tiff knew.

She smiled and said to him quietly, 'Yeah, I have a feeling we aren't finished yet.'

Author's note

'Think occasionally of the suffering of which
you spare yourself the sight.'

Albert Schweitzer

I hope you have enjoyed reading Toby's story. It is a story I
believe needed to be told for many reasons.

Firstly, because it is such an incredible tale. I still
remember my first time hearing it. Tiff and I met at the
local playgroup. I had horses myself and Tiff was still in
the Mounties, so between our horses, dogs and children,
we had a lot in common. One day we were driving back
to Bilpin from a shopping expedition in Lithgow and were
talking about horses and Tiffany's work when she mentioned that Toby and Bundy were brothers. She then told
me a highly abridged version of the story that you have
just read. When she finished, a shiver went down my spine.
I couldn't believe that something so fantastic had actually

285

happened and that nobody thought it extraordinary. Even Tiffany was quite blasé about it.

I asked her permission to write this book and when I finally got the chance to put pen to paper, I was again astounded, this time by the richness of some of the details that Tiff had omitted in her original account: Toby's infection, saving the German tourist, Sid the stockman and throwing Julia at the police stables.

Then I met Toby, and I knew I had to tell his story. He was already a legend in my mind, and he didn't disappoint in real life. He had no problem with me, a perfect stranger, hugging and kissing him and there was so much to hug. Every part of him was huge: a huge head, neck and body but most of all heart. He oozed softness, kindness and benevolence but I could also see a cheeky glint in his eye. That was ten years ago, and I love him even more today than I did back then. It has truly been a remarkable experience to unfurl and document this wonderful horse's life.

But while it is an amazing story, that was not the only thing that drew me to it.

As an animal lover I have alternated between despair and hope for most of my life. Probably more despair than hope, to be honest.

It took me a long time to understand how people can turn a blind eye to suffering. How cognitive dissonance can turn a normally kind person into an abettor of evil.

How we switch off from cruelty every single day, allowing it to invade our psyche. And how, when no one questions it, it then becomes ingrained as the norm. We are too scared, too desensitised and too conditioned to speak up, to confront the perpetrators or rescue the abused.

Except in rare examples like this.

What I saw in this story was a woman who allowed herself to *feel* and to *act*. Who didn't switch off, who didn't ignore. She could have so easily forgotten Toby once she left him behind, but she didn't. She went back and saved him and gave him a second chance.

And then, like so many rescued animals, he repaid her kindness a thousand times over.

Toby could have so easily ended up with a bullet between his eyes and we would have been none the wiser, but consider what we would have missed. It's heartbreaking to think of how many other beautiful creatures are lost each day that we aren't even aware of. They too might have changed the life of an individual or, like Toby, hundreds of lives.

Toby's story gave me a rare moment of hope. That there *are* ordinary people out there doing extraordinary things. That cruelty and indifference need not be the norm and that kindness and compassion can triumph. But for this to happen we need to normalise kindness. We need to recognise it in ourselves and others and we need to encourage it to flourish. By sharing Toby's story, I hope to contribute to a conversation that celebrates unconditional kindness for all living souls.

So, what is Toby doing now?

After he retired, Toby moved to Bilpin and became a member of Tiff's family. He met their other horses and ponies and reunited with Bundy, who had also retired after a successful competitive career.

Toby's lameness gradually subsided without the constant pressure of daily patrols on hard surfaces. It did take a little time for him to adjust to the lack of structure after so many years in the Police Force but eventually he embraced the carefree lifestyle, grew his hair long and became a regular horse.

He continued in his role as a teacher, teaching various friends and family to ride. Doing just enough work to keep his joints subtle and mind active, all the while enjoying life on the scenic edge of Wollemi National Park. But he has had a few dramas, with him needing to be evacuated as bushfires engulfed the tiny mountain township of Bilpin in 2019. He also became a member of Kurrajong Pony Club, taking Tiff's son Kye for a number of years. While Toby's love of adults was always obvious, his love for children also became apparent during this time.

Now in his mid-twenties, he is happy and healthy and still very much the same. A wonderful mélange of eccentricity. A kind, confident, gloriously funny individual whose story touched my heart and I hope has warmed yours.

Acknowledgements

Second Chance has been a long time coming. Fifteen years, to be exact.

What started out as a short story I felt compelled to write evolved into this book, and along the way a host of people have contributed in so many ways.

First and foremost, Tiffany Williams, for trusting me with her and Toby's story. Of course, in true Tiffany style, she didn't think twice when I asked her if I could write it. I still remember the afternoons we sat in the sun and chatted about the events in the book, while I took notes and our kids played. This friendship of the past sixteen years has been a crazy, wild ride and I wouldn't have missed it for the world.

I would also like to give my heartfelt thanks to the following people:

My dear friend Randi Rotne. You were the first person to read the short story and tell me you liked it. I had no idea at that point what the story would become, but your reaction gave me a glimpse of what could be.

My friend Laura Laidlaw, who edited that short story.

Zoe Naylor, for reigniting the spark. The story had sat for twelve years until you gave me the impetus to revisit, review and create what it is today.

My sisters and brother, Margi, Bruce and Helen, for your love and support, not just with this book but always.

Sandy Wright and Eleanor Hogan, for your advice during the submission process.

Another old friend and my writing buddy, Linda Atkins. I'm not sure what I would have done without your support and advice these past few years.

Nadia Batton, for your lovely contribution to Toby's story and for your beautiful photographs.

Don Eyb OAM and the New South Wales Mounted Police Unit for your assistance in the final stages of the manuscript.

Tom, Kylie, Tessa and Sam from Allen & Unwin, and also freelance editor Susan, who have helped me on my publishing journey and made it an amazing experience.

Shai Desai and David Myers from Learning Plan, for your constant support all these years and flexibility in allowing me to complete the editing process.

And finally my children, Kelsea, Kyle and Alana. You have enriched my life simply by your being. I am a better person for knowing you, and you have taught me more than you will ever know.